W9-AUN-189

The Guide to Clinical Preventive Services

2007

Recommendations of the
U.S. Preventive Services Task Force

AHRQ
Agency for Healthcare Research and Quality
Advancing Excellence in Health Care • www.ahrq.gov

The recommendation statements in this *Guide* are abridged. To view the full recommendation statements or recommendation statements published after 2006, go to **http://www.ahrq.gov/clinic/uspstf/uspstopics.htm.**

The U.S Preventive Services Task Force's (USPSTF) **Electronic Preventive Services Selector (ePSS)** allows users to download the USPSTF recommendations to PDA devices, receive PDA e-mail notifications of updates, and search and browse recommendations online. Users can search the ePSS for recommendations by patient age, sex, and pregnancy status. To download, subscribe, or search, go to **http://epss.ahrq.gov.**

Recommendations made by the USPSTF are independent of the U.S. Government. They should not be construed as an official position of AHRQ or the U.S. Department of Health and Human Services.

Foreword

The Agency for Healthcare Research and Quality (AHRQ) is pleased to present *The Guide to Clinical Preventive Services 2007*, the annually updated pocket guide that puts evidence-based, "gold-standard" recommendations from the U.S. Preventive Services Task Force (USPSTF) at your fingertips. The 2007 *Guide* offers recommendations on 58 clinical preventive services made by the Task Force from 2001 to 2006.

Partners who have helped to promote and to distribute the *Guide* have been key to our successes to date. In 2006, the United Health Foundation and AHRQ entered into a partnership that allowed 430,000 copies of the 2006 USPSTF *Guide to Clinical Preventive Services* to be distributed to clinicians nationwide. This partnership put a valuable preventive care tool in the hands of providers, including internists, family physicians, pediatricians, osteopathic physicians, and nurse practitioners, who could best use it to maximize services to their patients.

The USPSTF recommendations are being used every day in health care settings to improve clinical practice. For example, based on a very successful pilot project, the Harris County Hospital District in Houston, Texas—the fourth-largest hospital district in the United States—used recommendations and related materials as part of a preventive services protocol in all 12 of its community health centers. In addition to its community health centers, Harris County Hospital

District includes a school-based, mobile, and homeless program that reaches a population of more than 300,000 people.

We are also pleased that the *Guide* is being used to train new generations of clinicians. Graduate nurse practitioner students at the Kent State University School of Nursing have received an introduction to clinical prevention, which includes an overview of the Task Force, its history, and its goals. The school's electronic nursing syllabus provides a direct link to the *Guide*. The school also uses USPSTF screening and counseling recommendations as the basis for students' clinical assessments.

The recommendations and clinical considerations in the *Guide* can help you work with your patients to make better-informed decisions about preventive services. This is a key step that clinicians can take to help their patients remain healthy and to improve the quality of our health care system.

Carolyn M. Clancy, M.D.
Director
Agency for Healthcare Research and Quality

Preface

Since its inception 22 years ago, the U.S. Preventive Services Task Force (USPSTF) has been dedicated to: 1) evaluating the benefits of primary and secondary preventive services in apparently healthy persons based on age, sex, and risk factors for disease, and 2) making recommendations about which preventive services should be incorporated into primary care practice. While the intended audience for these recommendations continues to be primary care clinicians, the reach of the Task Force has expanded over time: recommendations of the USPSTF are now considered by many to provide definitive standards for preventive services, informing recommendations developed by professional societies, coverage policies of many health plans and insurers, health care quality measures, and national health objectives.

USPSTF methods have evolved to incorporate not only the quality of evidence supporting a specific preventive service, but also the magnitude of net benefit (benefits minus harms) in providing the service. Each recommendation is based on a rigorous review of the evidence involving a series of steps:

- Creation of an analytic framework and a set of key questions that determine the scope of the literature review.

- Systematic review of the relevant literature to answer the key questions.

- Quality rating of bodies of literature supporting each key question, as well as the quality and certainty of the evidence overall.

- Estimation of benefits and harms.

- Determination of the balance of benefits and harms of the service, or net benefit.

The recommendation is then linked to a letter grade that reflects the magnitude of net benefit and the strength and certainty of the evidence supporting the provision of a specific preventive service. The recommendation is graded from "A" (strongly recommended) to "D" (recommended against). The Task Force gives an "I" recommendation when the evidence is insufficient to determine net benefit.

The USPSTF realizes that clinical decisions about patients involve more complex considerations than the evidence alone; clinicians should always understand the evidence but individualize decision-making to the specific patient and situation. The Clinical Considerations section of each USPSTF Recommendation Statement helps clinicians implement the recommendations by offering practical information so they can tailor these recommendations to individual patients. The USPSTF suggests that clinicians:

- Discuss services with **"A" and "B" recommendations** with eligible patients and offer them as a priority.

- Discourage the use of services with **"D" recommendations** unless there are unusual additional considerations.

- Give lower priority to services with **"C" recommendations;** they need not be provided unless there are individual considerations in favor of providing the service.

- For services with **"I" recommendations,** carefully read the Clinical Considerations section for guidance, and help patients understand the uncertainty surrounding these services.

The Guide to Clinical Preventive Services 2007 is a compilation of abridged USPSTF recommendations released from 2001 through 2006 and can be used as an evidence-based tool at the point of patient care. Some recommendations have been updated from those made by the USPSTF in1996, while others address preventive services not previously considered by the USPSTF. The complete USPSTF recommendation statements are available along with their supporting scientific evidence at http://www.ahrq.gov/clinic/uspstf/uspstopics.htm. In addition, the USPSTF Electronic Preventive Services Selector (ePSS), available via PDA or on the Web at

http://epss.ahrq.gov, allows users to search USPSTF
recommendations by patient age and other clinical
characteristics.

I hope you find *The Guide to Clinical Preventive
Services 2007* to be a useful tool as you care for
patients.

Ned Calonge, M.D., M.P.H.
Chair, U.S. Preventive Services Task Force

Contents

Contents

*Recommendations new in 2006.

Section 1.

Preventive Services Recommended by the USPSTF

All recommendation statements in this Guide are abridged. To see the full recommendation statements and recommendations published after 2006, go to http://www.ahrq.gov/clinic/uspstf/uspstopics.htm.

Preventive Services Recommended by the USPSTF

The U.S. Preventive Services Task Force (USPSTF) recommends that clinicians discuss these preventive services with eligible patients and offer them as a priority. All these services have received an "A" (strongly recommended) or a "B" (recommended) grade from the Task Force.

For definitions of all grades used by the USPSTF, see the inside front cover. The full listings of all USPSTF recommendations for adults and children are in Section 2 (P. 9) and Section 3 (P. 179).

Recommendation	Adults		Special Populations	
	Men	Women	Pregnant Women	Children
Abdominal Aortic Aneurysm, Screening[1]	✓			
Alcohol Misuse Screening and Behavioral Counseling Interventions	✓	✓	✓	
Aspirin for the Primary Prevention of Cardiovascular Events[2]	✓	✓		
Bacteriuria, Screening for Asymptomatic			✓	
Breast Cancer, Chemoprevention[3]		✓		

continued

3

Preventive Services Recommended by the USPSTF *(continued)*

Recommendation	Adults		Special Populations	
	Men	Women	Pregnant Women	Children
Breast Cancer, Screening[4]		✓		
Breast and Ovarian Cancer Susceptibility, Genetic Risk Assessment and BRCA Mutation Testing[5]		✓		
Breastfeeding, Behavioral Interventions to Promote[6]		✓	✓	
Cervical Cancer, Screening[7]		✓		
Chlamydial Infection, Screening[8]		✓	✓	
Colorectal Cancer, Screening[9]	✓	✓		
Dental Caries in Preschool Children, Prevention[10]				✓

continued

4

Recommendation	Adults		Special Populations	
	Men	Women	Pregnant Women	Children
Depression, Screening[11]	✓	✓		
Diabetes Mellitus in Adults, Screening for Type 2[12]	✓	✓		
Diet, Behavioral Counseling in Primary Care to Promote a Healthy[13]	✓	✓		
Gonorrhea, Screening[14]		✓	✓	
Gonorrhea, Prophylactic Medication[15]				✓
Hepatitis B Virus Infection, Screening[16]			✓	
High Blood Pressure, Screening	✓	✓		
HIV, Screening[17]	✓	✓	✓	✓
Iron Deficiency Anemia, Prevention[18]				✓
Iron Deficiency Anemia, Screening[19]			✓	

continued

Preventive Services Recommended by the USPSTF (continued)

Recommendation	Adults		Special Populations	
	Men	Women	Pregnant Women	Children
Lipid Disorders, Screening[20]	✓	✓		
Obesity in Adults, Screening[21]	✓	✓		
Osteoporosis in Postmenopausal Women, Screening[22]		✓		
Rh (D) Incompatibility, Screening[23]			✓	
Syphilis Infection, Screening[24]	✓	✓	✓	
Tobacco Use and Tobacco-Caused Disease, Counseling[25]	✓	✓	✓	
Visual Impairment in Children Younger than Age 5 Years, Screening[26]				✓

[1] One-time screening by ultrasonography in men aged 65 to 75 who have ever smoked.

[2] Adults at increased risk for coronary heart disease.

[3] Discuss with women at high risk for breast cancer and at low risk for adverse effects of chemoprevention.

[4] Mammography every 1-2 years for women 40 and older.

[5] Refer women whose family history is associated with an increased risk for deleterious mutations in BRCA1 or BRCA2 genes for genetic counseling and evaluation for BRCA testing.

[6] Structured education and behavioral counseling programs.

[7] Women who have been sexually active and have a cervix.

[8] Sexually active women 25 and younger and other asymptomatic women at increased risk for infection. Asymptomatic pregnant women 25 and younger and others at increased risk.

[9] Men and women 50 and older.

[10] Prescribe oral fluoride supplementation at currently recommended doses to preschool children older than 6 months whose primary water source is deficient in fluoride.

[11] In clinical practices with systems to assure accurate diagnoses, effective treatment, and follow-up.

[12] Adults with hypertension or hyperlipidemia.

[13] Adults with hyperlipidemia and other known risk factors for cardiovascular and diet-related chronic disease.

[14] All sexually active women, including those who are pregnant, at increased risk for infection (that is, if they are young or have other individual or population risk factors).

[15] Prophylactic ocular topical medication for all newborns against gonococcal ophthalmia neonatorum.

[16] Pregnant women at first prenatal visit.

7

[17] All adolescents and adults at increased risk for HIV infection and all pregnant women.

[18] Routine iron supplementation for asymptomatic children aged 6 to 12 months who are at increased risk for iron deficiency anemia.

[19] Routine screening in asymptomatic pregnant women.

[20] Men 35 and older and women 45 and older. Younger adults with other risk factors for coronary disease. Screening for lipid disorders to include measurement of total cholesterol and high-density lipoprotein cholesterol.

[21] Intensive counseling and behavioral interventions to promote sustained weight loss for obese adults.

[22] Women 65 and older and women 60 and older at increased risk for osteoporotic fractures.

[23] Blood typing and antibody testing at first pregnancy-related visit. Repeated antibody testing for unsensitized Rh (D)-negative women at 24-28 weeks gestation unless biological father is known to be Rh (D) negative.

[24] Persons at increased risk and all pregnant women.

[25] Tobacco cessation interventions for those who use tobacco. Augmented pregnancy-tailored counseling to pregnant women who smoke.

[26] To detect amblyopia, strabismus, and defects in visual acuity.

Section 2.

Recommendations for Adults

All recommendation statements in this Guide are abridged. To see the full recommendation statements and recommendations published after 2006, go to http://www.ahrq.gov/clinic/uspstf/uspstopics.htm.

Cancer

Screening for Bladder Cancer in Adults

Summary of Recommendation

The U.S. Preventive Services Task Force (USPSTF) recommends against routine screening for bladder cancer in adults. *Rating: D Recommendation.*

Clinical Considerations

■ Bladder cancer is 2 to 3 times more common in men than in women and is unusual before age 50. Bladder cancer is heterogeneous; it is a spectrum of conditions, most of which are not life-threatening.

■ Screening tests—such as microscopic urinalysis, urine dipstick, urine cytology, or such new tests as bladder tumor antigen (BTA) or nuclear matrix protein (NMP22) immunoassay—can detect bladder cancers that are clinically unapparent. However, because of the low prevalence of bladder cancer, the positive predictive value of these tests is low.

■ Smoking increases the risk for bladder cancer; about 50% of all cases of bladder cancer occur in current or former smokers. Smokers should be counseled on quitting smoking.

11

- People in occupations that involve exposure to chemicals used in the dye or rubber industries may also have increased risk for bladder cancer. The USPSTF did not review the evidence for targeted screening for those with occupational exposure.

This USPSTF recommendation was first published by: Agency for Healthcare Research and Quality, Rockville, MD. June 2004. http://www.ahrq.gov/clinic/3rduspstf/bladder/blacanrs.htm.

Genetic Risk Assessment and BRCA Mutation Testing for Breast and Ovarian Cancer Susceptibility

Summary of Recommendations

The U.S. Preventive Services Task Force (USPSTF) recommends against routine referral for genetic counseling or routine breast cancer susceptibility gene *(BRCA)* testing for women whose family history is not associated with an increased risk for deleterious mutations in breast cancer susceptibility gene 1 *(BRCA1)* or breast cancer susceptibility gene 2 *(BRCA2)*. *Rating: D Recommendation.*

The USPSTF recommends that women whose family history is associated with an increased risk for deleterious mutations in *BRCA1* or *BRCA2* genes be referred for genetic counseling and evaluation for *BRCA* testing. *Rating: B Recommendation.*

Clinical Considerations

■ These recommendations apply to women who have not received a diagnosis of breast or ovarian cancer. They do not apply to women with a family history of breast or ovarian cancer that includes a relative with a known deleterious mutation in *BRCA1* or *BRCA2* genes; these women should be referred for genetic counseling. These recommendations do not apply to men.

13

■ Although there currently are no standardized referral criteria, women with an increased-risk family history should be considered for genetic counseling to further evaluate their potential risks.

■ Certain specific family history patterns are associated with an increased risk for deleterious mutations in the *BRCA1* or *BRCA2* gene. Both maternal and paternal family histories are important. For non-Ashkenazi Jewish women, these patterns include 2 first-degree relatives with breast cancer, 1 of whom received the diagnosis at age 50 years or younger; a combination of 3 or more first- or second-degree relatives with breast cancer regardless of age at diagnosis; a combination of both breast and ovarian cancer among first- and second-degree relatives; a first-degree relative with bilateral breast cancer; a combination of 2 or more first- or second-degree relatives with ovarian cancer regardless of age at diagnosis; a first- or second-degree relative with both breast and ovarian cancer at any age; and a history of breast cancer in a male relative.

■ For women of Ashkenazi Jewish heritage, an increased-risk family history includes any first-degree relative (or 2 second-degree relatives on the same side of the family) with breast or ovarian cancer.

■ About 2 percent of adult women in the general population have an increased-risk family history as defined here. Women with none of these family history patterns have a low probability of having a deleterious mutation in *BRCA1* or *BRCA2* genes.

14

■ Computational tools are available to predict the risk for clinically important *BRCA* mutations (that is, *BRCA* mutations associated with the presence of breast cancer, ovarian cancer, or both), but these tools have not been verified in the general population. There is no empirical evidence concerning the level of risk for a *BRCA* mutation that merits referral for genetic counseling.

■ Not all women with a potentially deleterious *BRCA* mutation will develop breast or ovarian cancer. In a woman who has a clinically important *BRCA* mutation, the probability of developing breast or ovarian cancer by age 70 years is estimated to be 35 percent to 84 percent for breast cancer and 10 percent to 50 percent for ovarian cancer.

■ Appropriate genetic counseling helps women make informed decisions, can improve their knowledge and perception of absolute risk for breast and ovarian cancer, and can often reduce anxiety. Genetic counseling includes elements of counseling; risk assessment; pedigree analysis; and, in some cases, recommendations for testing for *BRCA* mutations in affected family members, the presenting patient, or both. It is best delivered by a suitably trained health care provider.

■ A *BRCA* test is typically ordered by a physician. When done in concert with genetic counseling, the test assures the linkage of testing with appropriate management decisions. Genetic testing may lead to potential adverse ethical, legal, and social consequences, such as insurance and employment discrimination; these issues should be discussed in the context of genetic counseling and evaluation for testing.

■ Among women with *BRCA1* or *BRCA2* mutations, prophylactic mastectomy or oophorectomy decreases the incidence of breast and ovarian cancer; there is inadequate evidence for mortality benefits. Chemoprevention with selective estrogen receptor modulators may decrease incidence of estrogen receptor-positive breast cancer; however, it is also associated with adverse effects, such as pulmonary embolism, deep venous thrombosis, and endometrial cancer. Most breast cancer associated with *BRCA1* mutations is estrogen receptor-negative and thus is not prevented by tamoxifen. Intensive screening with mammography has poor sensitivity, and there is no evidence of benefit of intensive screening for women with *BRCA1* or *BRCA2* gene mutations. Magnetic resonance imaging (MRI) may detect more cases of cancer, but the effect on mortality is not clear.

■ Women with an increased-risk family history are at risk not only for deleterious *BRCA1* or *BRCA2* mutations but potentially for other unknown mutations as well. Women with an increased-risk family history who have negative results on tests for *BRCA1* and *BRCA2* mutations may also benefit from surgical prophylaxis.

This USPSTF recommendation was first published in *Ann Intern Med.* 2005;143:355-361.

Chemoprevention of Breast Cancer

Summary of Recommendations

The U.S. Preventive Services Task Force (USPSTF) recommends against routine use of tamoxifen or raloxifene for the primary prevention of breast cancer in women at low or average risk for breast cancer. (See Clinical Considerations for a discussion of risk.) *Rating: D Recommendation.*

The USPSTF recommends that clinicians discuss chemoprevention with women at high risk for breast cancer and at low risk for adverse effects of chemoprevention. (See Clinical Considerations for a discussion of risk.) Clinicians should inform patients of the potential benefits and harms of chemoprevention. *Rating: B Recommendation.*

Clinical Considerations

■ Clinicians should consider both the risk for breast cancer and the risk for adverse effects when identifying women who may be candidates for chemoprevention.

Risk for breast cancer. Older age; a family history of breast cancer in a mother, sister, or daughter; and a history of atypical hyperplasia on a breast biopsy are the strongest risk factors for breast cancer. Table 1 indicates how the estimated benefits of tamoxifen vary depending on age and family history. Other factors that contribute to risk include race, early age at menarche, pregnancy history (nulliparity or older

17

age at first birth), and number of breast biopsies. The risk for developing breast cancer within the next 5 years can be estimated using risk factor information by completing the National Cancer Institute Breast Cancer Risk Tool (the "Gail model," available at http://cancer.gov/bcrisktool/ or 800-4-CANCER). Clinicians can use this information to help individual patients considering tamoxifen therapy estimate the potential benefit. However, the validity, feasibility, and impact of using the Gail model to identify appropriate candidates for chemoprevention have not been tested in a primary care setting. The Gail model does not incorporate estradiol levels or estrogen use, factors that some studies suggest may influence the effectiveness of tamoxifen.

Risk for adverse effects. Women are at lower risk for adverse effects from chemoprevention if they are younger; have no predisposition to thromboembolic events such as stroke, pulmonary embolism, or deep venous thrombosis; or do not have a uterus.

■ In general, the balance of benefits and harms of chemoprevention is more favorable for:

1. Women in their 40s who are at increased risk for breast cancer and have no predisposition to thromboembolic events.

2. Women in their 50s who are at increased risk for breast cancer, have no predisposition to thromboembolic events, and do not have a uterus. For example, a woman who is 45 years of

age and has a mother, sister, or daughter with breast cancer would have approximately a 1.6 percent risk for developing breast cancer over the next 5 years (Table 1). On average, treating such women with tamoxifen for 5 years would prevent about three times as many invasive cancers (8 per 1,000) as the number of serious thromboembolic complications caused (1 stroke and 1 to 2 pulmonary emboli per 1,000). Among women 55 years of age, benefits exceed harms only for those who are not at risk for endometrial cancer; and the margin of benefit is small unless risk for breast cancer is substantially increased (for example, 4% over 5 years).

■ Women younger than 40 years of age have a lower risk for breast cancer, and thus will not experience as large an absolute benefit from breast cancer chemoprevention as older women. Women 60 years of age and older, who have the highest risk for breast cancer also have the highest risk for complications from chemoprevention, with a less favorable balance of benefits and harms.

■ The USPSTF found more evidence for the benefits of tamoxifen than for the benefits of raloxifene. Currently, only tamoxifen is approved by the U.S. Food and Drug Administration (FDA) for the specific indication of breast cancer chemoprevention. Although there are biological reasons to suspect that raloxifene should have similar benefits, trial data currently are limited to

19

Table 1. Predicted Benefits and Harms of 5 Years of Tamoxifen Therapy According to Age and Family History[1]

Variable[2]	Women 45 Years of Age	Women 55 Years of Age	Women 65 Years of Age	Women 75 Years of Age
Predicted 5-year risk of breast cancer, %[3]				
No family history	0.7	1.1	1.5	1.6
Family history	1.6	2.3	3.2	3.4
Benefits per 1,000 women over 5 y of tamoxifen therapy				
Cases of invasive breast cancer avoided, n				
No family history	3-4	5-6	7-8	8
Family history	8	11-12	16	17
Cases of noninvasive breast cancer avoided, n				
No family history	1-2	2	2-3	2-3
Family history	2-3	3-4	4-5	5-6

continued

20

Variable[2]	Women 45 Years of Age	Women 55 Years of Age	Women 65 Years of Age	Women 75 Years of Age
Hip fractures avoided, n[4]	<1	3	5	15
Harms per 1000 women over 5 y of tamoxifen therapy				
Cases of endometrial cancer caused, n[4]	1-2	12	21	22
Strokes caused, n[4]	1	3	9	20
Pulmonary emboli caused, n[4]	1-2	4-5	9	18
Cases of deep venous thrombosis caused, n[4]	1-2	1-2	3	4

[1]These estimates are based on the Gail model, outcomes from the Breast Cancer Prevention Trial, and baseline rates of harms from Gail et al.[1]

[2]No family history = no first-degree relatives with breast cancer; family history = 1 first-degree relative with breast cancer.

[3]Based on menarche at 12 years of age, first birth at 22 years of age, and no history of breast biopsy, as calculated from the Gail model.

[4]Modified from Gail et al.[1]

21

one study in which the primary outcome was fracture prevention. Additional trials to further evaluate this drug's efficacy for breast cancer chemoprevention are underway, including a trial comparing efficacy and safety of raloxifene and tamoxifen. Raloxifene is approved by the FDA for preventing and treating osteoporosis.

Reference

1. Gail MH, Costantino JH, Bryant J, et al. Weighing the risks and benefits of tamoxifen treatment for preventing breast cancer. *J Natl Cancer Inst.* 1999;91:1829-1846.

This USPSTF recommendation was first published in: *Ann Intern Med.* 2002; 137(1):56-58.

Screening for Breast Cancer

Summary of Recommendations

The U.S. Preventive Services Task Force (USPSTF) recommends screening mammography, with or without clinical breast examination (CBE), every 1-2 years for women aged 40 and older. *Rating: B Recommendation.*

The USPSTF concludes that the evidence is insufficient to recommend for or against routine CBE alone to screen for breast cancer. *Rating: I Recommendation.*

The USPSTF concludes that the evidence is insufficient to recommend for or against teaching or performing routine breast self-examination (BSE). *Rating: I Recommendation.*

Clinical Considerations

- The precise age at which the benefits from screening mammography justify the potential harms is a subjective judgment and should take into account patient preferences. Clinicians should inform women about the potential benefits (reduced chance of dying from breast cancer), potential harms (e.g., false-positive results, unnecessary biopsies), and limitations of the test that apply to women their age. Clinicians should tell women that the balance of benefits and potential harms of mammography improves with increasing age for women between the ages of 40 and 70.

■ Women who are at increased risk for breast cancer (e.g., those with a family history of breast cancer in a mother or sister, a previous breast biopsy revealing atypical hyperplasia, or first childbirth after age 30) are more likely to benefit from regular mammography than women at lower risk. The recommendation for women to begin routine screening in their 40s is strengthened by a family history of breast cancer having been diagnosed before menopause.

■ The USPSTF did not examine whether women should be screened for genetic mutations (e.g., *BRCA1* and *BRCA2*) that increase the risk for developing breast cancer, or whether women with genetic mutations might benefit from earlier or more frequent screening for breast cancer.

■ In the trials that demonstrated the effectiveness of mammography in lowering breast cancer mortality, screening was performed every 12-33 months. For women aged 50 and older, there is little evidence to suggest that annual mammography is more effective than mammography done every other year. For women aged 40-49, available trials also have not reported a clear advantage of annual mammography over biennial mammography. Nevertheless, some experts recommend annual mammography based on the lower sensitivity of the test and on evidence that tumors grow more rapidly in this age group.

■ The precise age at which to discontinue screening mammography is uncertain. Only 2 randomized controlled trials enrolled women older than 69 and no trials enrolled women older than 74. Older women face a higher probability of developing and dying from breast cancer but also have a greater chance of dying from other causes. Women with comorbid conditions that limit their life expectancy are unlikely to benefit from screening.

- Clinicians should refer patients to mammography screening centers with proper accreditation and quality assurance standards to ensure accurate imaging and radiographic interpretation. Clinicians should adopt office systems to ensure timely and adequate follow-up of abnormal results. A listing of accredited facilities is available at http://www.fda.gov/cdrh/mammography/certified. html.

- Clinicians who advise women to perform BSE or who perform routine CBE to screen for breast cancer should understand that there is currently insufficient evidence to determine whether these practices affect breast cancer mortality, and that they are likely to increase the incidence of clinical assessments and biopsies.

This USPSTF recommendation was first published in: *Ann Intern Med.* 2002; 137 (Part 1):344-346.

Screening for Cervical Cancer

Summary of Recommendations

The U.S. Preventive Services Task Force (USPSTF) strongly recommends screening for cervical cancer in women who have been sexually active and have a cervix. *Rating: A Recommendation.*

The USPSTF recommends against routinely screening women older than age 65 for cervical cancer if they have had adequate recent screening with normal Pap smears and are not otherwise at high risk for cervical cancer (go to *Clinical Considerations*). *Rating: D Recommendation.*

The USPSTF recommends against routine Pap smear screening in women who have had a total hysterectomy for benign disease. *Rating: D Recommendation.*

The USPSTF concludes that the evidence is insufficient to recommend for or against the routine use of new technologies to screen for cervical cancer. *Rating: I Recommendation.*

The USPSTF concludes that the evidence is insufficient to recommend for or against the routine use of human papillomavirus (HPV) testing as a primary screening test for cervical cancer. *Rating: I Recommendation.*

Clinical Considerations

■ The goal of cytologic screening is to sample the transformation zone, the area where physiologic transformation from columnar endocervical epithelium to squamous (ectocervical) epithelium takes place and where dysplasia and cancer arise. A meta-analysis of randomized trials supports the combined use of an extended tip spatula to sample the ectocervix and a cytobrush to sample the endocervix.[1]

■ The optimal age to begin screening is unknown. Data on natural history of HPV infection and the incidence of high-grade lesions and cervical cancer suggest that screening can safely be delayed until 3 years after onset of sexual activity or until age 21, whichever comes first.[2] Although there is little value in screening women who have never been sexually active, many U.S. organizations recommend routine screening by age 18 or 21 for all women, based on the generally high prevalence of sexual activity by that age in the U.S. and concerns that clinicians may not always obtain accurate sexual histories.

■ Discontinuation of cervical cancer screening in older women is appropriate, provided women have had adequate recent screening with normal Pap results. The optimal age to discontinue screening is not clear, but risk of cervical cancer and yield of screening decline steadily through middle age. The USPSTF found evidence that yield of screening was low in previously screened women after age 65. New

American Cancer Society (ACS) recommendations suggest stopping cervical cancer screening at age 70. Screening is recommended in older women who have not been previously screened, when information about previous screening is unavailable, or when screening is unlikely to have occurred in the past (e.g., among women from countries without screening programs). Evidence is limited to define "adequate recent screening." The ACS guidelines recommend that older women who have had three or more documented, consecutive, technically satisfactory normal/negative cervical cytology tests, and who have had no abnormal/positive cytology tests within the last 10 years, can safely stop screening.[2]

■ The USPSTF found no direct evidence that annual screening achieves better outcomes than screening every 3 years. Modeling studies suggest little added benefit of more frequent screening for most women. The majority of cervical cancers in the United States occur in women who have never been screened or who have not been screened within the past 5 years; additional cases occur in women who do not receive appropriate follow-up after an abnormal Pap smear.[3,4] Because sensitivity of a single Pap test for high-grade lesions may only be 60-80%, however, most organizations in the United States recommend that annual Pap smears be performed until a specified number (usually two or three) are cytologically normal before lengthening the screening interval.[5] The ACS guidelines suggest waiting until age 30 before lengthening the screening interval[2]; the American College of Obstetricians and Gynecologists (ACOG) identifies additional risk factors that might justify annual screening, including a history of cervical neoplasia, infection with HPV or other sexually transmitted diseases (STDs), or high-risk sexual behavior,[7] but data are limited to determine the benefits of these strategies.[7]

- Discontinuation of cytological screening after total hysterectomy for benign disease (e.g., no evidence of cervical neoplasia or cancer) is appropriate given the low yield of screening and the potential harms from false-positive results in this population.[7,8] Clinicians should confirm that a total hysterectomy was performed (through surgical records or inspecting for absence of a cervix); screening may be appropriate when the indications for hysterectomy are uncertain. ACS and ACOG recommend continuing cytologic screening after hysterectomy for women with a history of invasive cervical cancer or DES exposure due to increased risk for vaginal neoplasms, but data on the yield of such screening are sparse.

- A majority of cases of invasive cervical cancer occur in women who are not adequately screened.[3,4] Clinicians, hospitals, and health plans should develop systems to identify and screen the subgroup of women who have had no screening or who have had inadequate past screening.

■ Newer Food and Drug Administration (FDA)-approved technologies, such as the liquid-based cytology (e.g., ThinPrep®), may have improved sensitivity over conventional Pap smear screening, but at a considerably higher cost and possibly with lower specificity. Even if sensitivity is improved, modeling studies suggest these methods are not likely to be cost-effective unless used with screening intervals of 3 years or longer. Liquid-based cytology permits testing of specimens for HPV, which may be useful in guiding management of women whose Pap smear reveals atypical squamous cells. HPV DNA testing for primary cervical cancer screening has not been approved by the FDA and its role in screening remains uncertain.

References

1. Martin-Hirsch P, Lilford R, Jarvis G, Kitchener HC. Efficacy of cervical-smear collection devices: a systematic review and meta-analysis [published erratum appears in *Lancet*. 2000 Jan 29;355(9201):414]. *Lancet*. 1999;354(9192):1763-1770.

2. Smith RA, Cokkinides V, von Eschenbach AC, et al. American Cancer Society Guideline for the Early Detection of Cervical Neoplasia and Cancer. *CA Cancer J Clin*. 2002;52(1):8-22.

3. Hildesheim A, Hadjimichael O, Schwartz PE, et al. Risk factors for rapid-onset cervical cancer. *Am J Obstet Gynecol*. 1999;180(3 Pt 1):571-577.

4. Janerich DT, Hadjimichael O, Schwartz PE, et al. The screening histories of women with invasive cervical cancer, Connecticut. *Am J Public Health.* 1995;85(6):791-794.

5. Hartman KE, Hall SA, Nanda K, Boggess JF, Zolnoun D. *Screening for Cervical Cancer.* Systematic Evidence Review. No. 25. (Prepared by the Research Triangle Institute-University of North Carolina Evidence-based Practice Center under contract No. 290-97-0011). Rockville, MD: Agency for Healthcare Research and Quality. January 2002. Available on the AHRQ Web site: at: www.ahrq.gov/clinic/serfiles.htm.

6. American College of Obstetricians and Gynecologists. *Guidelines for Women's Health Care.* 2nd ed. Washington, DC: ACOG;2002: 121-134, 140-141.

7. Mitchell HS, Giles GG. Cancer diagnosis after a report of negative cervical cytology. *Med J Aust.* 1996;164(5):270-273.

8. Sigurdsson K. Trends in cervical intra-epithelial neoplasia in Iceland through 1995: evaluation of targeted age groups and screening intervals. *Acta Obstet Gynecol Scand.* 1999;78(6):486-492.

This USPSTF recommendation was first published by: Agency for Healthcare Research and Quality, Rockville, MD. January 2003. http://www.ahrq.gov/clinic/uspstf/uspscerv.htm.

Screening for Colorectal Cancer

Summary of Recommendation

The U.S. Preventive Services Task Force (USPSTF) strongly recommends that clinicians screen men and women 50 years of age or older for colorectal cancer. *Rating: A Recommendation.*

Clinical Considerations

- Potential screening options for colorectal cancer include home fecal occult blood testing (FOBT), flexible sigmoidoscopy, the combination of home FOBT and flexible sigmoidoscopy, colonoscopy, and double-contrast barium enema. Each option has advantages and disadvantages that may vary for individual patients and practice settings. The choice of specific screening strategy should be based on patient preferences, medical contraindications, patient adherence, and available resources for testing and follow-up. Clinicians should talk to patients about the benefits and potential harms associated with each option before selecting a screening strategy.

- The optimal interval for screening depends on the test. Annual FOBT offers greater reductions in mortality rates than biennial screening but produces more false-positive results. A 10-year interval has been recommended for colonoscopy on the basis of evidence regarding the natural history of adenomatous polyps. Shorter intervals (5 years) have been recommended for flexible sigmoidoscopy and double-contrast barium enema because of their lower sensitivity, but there is no direct evidence with which to determine the optimal interval for tests other than FOBT. Case-control studies have suggested that sigmoidoscopy every 10 years may be as effective as sigmoidoscopy performed at shorter intervals.

■ The USPSTF recommends initiating screening at 50 years of age for men and women at average risk for colorectal cancer, based on the incidence of cancer above this age in the general population. In persons at higher risk (for example, those with a first-degree relative who receives a diagnosis with colorectal cancer before 60 years of age), initiating screening at an earlier age is reasonable.

■ Expert guidelines exist for screening very high-risk patients, including those with a history suggestive of familial polyposis or hereditary nonpolyposis colorectal cancer, or those with a personal history of ulcerative colitis.[1] Early screening with colonoscopy may be appropriate, and genetic counseling or testing may be indicated for patients with genetic syndromes.

■ The appropriate age at which colorectal cancer screening should be discontinued is not known. Screening studies have generally been restricted to patients younger than 80 years of age, with colorectal cancer mortality rates beginning to decrease within 5 years of initiating screening. Yield of screening should increase in older persons (because of higher incidence of colorectal cancer), but benefits may be limited as a result of competing causes of death. Discontinuing screening is therefore reasonable in patients whose age or comorbid conditions limit life expectancy.

■ Proven methods of FOBT screening use guaiac-based test cards prepared at home by patients from three consecutive stool samples and forwarded to the clinician. Whether patients need to restrict their diet and avoid certain medications is not established. Rehydration of the specimens before testing increases the sensitivity of FOBT but substantially increases the number of false-positive test results. Neither digital rectal examination (DRE) nor the testing of a single stool specimen obtained during DRE is recommended as an adequate screening strategy for colorectal cancer.

■ The combination of FOBT and sigmoidoscopy may detect more cancers and more large polyps than either test alone, but the additional benefits and potential harms of combining the 2 tests are uncertain. In general, FOBT should precede sigmoidoscopy because a positive test result is an indication for colonoscopy, obviating the need for sigmoidoscopy.

■ Colonoscopy is the most sensitive and specific test for detecting cancer and large polyps but is associated with higher risks than other screening tests for colorectal cancer. These include a small risk for bleeding and risk for perforation, primarily associated with removal of polyps or biopsies performed during screening. Colonoscopy also usually requires more highly trained personnel, overnight bowel preparation, sedation, and longer recovery time, which may necessitate transportation for the patient. It is not certain whether the potential added benefits of colonoscopy relative to screening alternatives are large enough to justify the added risks and inconvenience for all patients.

■ Initial costs of colonoscopy are higher than the costs of other tests. Estimates of cost-effectiveness, however, suggest that, from a societal perspective, compared with no screening, all methods of colorectal cancer screening are likely to be as cost-effective as many other clinical preventive services-less than $30,000 per additional year of life gained.

Reference

1. Winawer SJ, Fletcher RH, Miller L, Godlee F, Stolar MH, Mulrow CD, et al. Colorectal cancer screening: clinical guidelines and rationale. *Gastroenterology.* 1997;112:594-642.

This USPSTF recommendation was first published in: *Ann Intern Med.* 2002;137:129-131.

Lung Cancer Screening

Summary of Recommendation

The U.S. Preventive Services Task Force (USPSTF) concludes that the evidence is insufficient to recommend for or against screening asymptomatic persons for lung cancer with either low dose computerized tomography (LDCT), chest x-ray (CXR), sputum cytology, or a combination of these tests. *Rating: I Recommendation.*

Clinical Considerations

■ The benefit of screening for lung cancer has not been established in any group, including asymptomatic high-risk populations such as older smokers. The balance of harms and benefits becomes increasingly unfavorable for persons at lower risk, such as nonsmokers.

■ The sensitivity of LDCT for detecting lung cancer is 4 times greater than the sensitivity of CXR. However, LDCT is also associated with a greater number of false-positive results, more radiation exposure, and increased costs compared with CXR.

■ Because of the high rate of false-positive results, many patients will undergo invasive diagnostic procedures as a result of lung cancer screening. Although the morbidity and mortality rates from these procedures in asymptomatic individuals are not available, mortality rates due to complications from surgical interventions in symptomatic patients reportedly range from 1.3% to 11.6%; morbidity rates range from 8.8% to 44%, with higher rates associated with larger resections.

■ Other potential harms of screening are potential anxiety and concern as a result of false-positive tests, as well as possible false reassurance because of false-negative results. However, these harms have not been adequately studied.

This USPSTF recommendation was first published in: *Ann Intern Med.* 2004;140:738-739.

Screening for Oral Cancer

Summary of Recommendation

The U.S. Preventive Services Task Force (USPSTF) concludes that the evidence is insufficient to recommend for or against routinely screening adults for oral cancer. *Rating: I Recommendation.*

Clinical Considerations

■ Direct inspection and palpation of the oral cavity is the most commonly recommended method of screening for oral cancer, although there are little data on the sensitivity and specificity of this method. Screening techniques other than inspection and palpation are being evaluated but are still experimental.

■ Tobacco use in all forms is the biggest risk factor for oral cancer. Alcohol abuse combined with tobacco use increases risk.

■ Clinicians should be alert to the possibility of oral cancer when treating patients who use tobacco or alcohol.

■ Patients should be encouraged to not use tobacco and to limit alcohol use in order to decrease their risk for oral cancer as well as heart disease, stroke, lung cancer, and cirrhosis.

This USPSTF recommendation was first published by: Agency for Healthcare Research and Quality, Rockville, MD. February 2004. http://www.ahrq.gov/clinic/3rduspstf/oralcan/oralcanrs.htm.

Screening for Ovarian Cancer

Summary of Recommendation

The U.S. Preventive Services Task Force (USPSTF) recommends against routine screening for ovarian cancer. *Rating: D Recommendation.*

Clinical Considerations

■ There is no existing evidence that any screening test, including CA-125, ultrasound, or pelvic examination, reduces mortality from ovarian cancer. Furthermore, existing evidence that screening can detect early-stage ovarian cancer is insufficient to indicate that this earlier diagnosis will reduce mortality.

■ Because there is a low incidence of ovarian cancer in the general population (age-adjusted incidence of 17 per 100,000 women), screening for ovarian cancer is likely to have a relatively low yield. The great majority of women with a positive screening test will not have ovarian cancer (ie, they will have a false-positive result). In women at average risk, the positive predictive value of an abnormal screening test is, at best, approximately 2% (ie, 98% of women with positive test results will not have ovarian cancer).

■ The positive predictive value of an initially positive screening test would be more favorable for women at higher risk. For example, the lifetime probability of ovarian cancer increases from about 1.6% in a

39

35-year-old woman without a family history of ovarian cancer to about 5% if she has 1 relative and 7% if she has 2 relatives with ovarian cancer. If ongoing clinical trials show that screening has a beneficial effect on mortality rates, then women at higher risk are likely to experience the greatest benefit.

This USPSTF recommendation was first published in: *Ann Fam Med.* 2004;2:260-262.

Screening for Pancreatic Cancer

Summary of Recommendation

The U.S. Preventive Services Task Force (USPSTF) recommends against routine screening for pancreatic cancer in asymptomatic adults using abdominal palpation, ultrasonography, or serologic markers. *Rating: D Recommendation.*

Clinical Considerations

■ Due to the poor prognosis of those diagnosed with pancreatic cancer, there is an interest in primary prevention. The evidence for diet-based prevention of pancreatic cancer is limited and conflicting. Some experts recommend lifestyle changes that may help to prevent pancreatic cancer, such as stopping the use of tobacco products, moderating alcohol intake, and eating a balanced diet with sufficient fruit and vegetables.

■ Persons with hereditary pancreatitis may have a higher lifetime risk for developing pancreatic cancer.[1] However, the USPSTF did not review the effectiveness of screening these patients.

41

Reference

1. Lowenfels AB, Maisonneuve P, DiMagno EP, et al.
   Hereditary pancreatitis and the risk of pancreatic
   cancer. International Hereditary Pancreatitis Study
   Group. *J Natl Cancer Inst.* 1997;89:442-446.

This USPSTF recommendation was first published by:
Agency for Healthcare Research and Quality, Rockville,
MD. February 2004. http://www.ahrq.gov/clinic/
3rduspstf/pancreatic/pancrers.htm.

Screening for Prostate Cancer

Summary of Recommendation

The U.S. Preventive Services Task Force (USPSTF) concludes that the evidence is insufficient to recommend for or against routine screening for prostate cancer using prostate specific antigen (PSA) testing or digital rectal examination (DRE). *Rating: I recommendation.*

Clinical Considerations

- Prostate specific antigen (PSA) testing and digital rectal examination (DRE) can effectively detect prostate cancer in its early pathologic stages. Recent evidence suggests that radical prostatectomy can reduce prostate cancer mortality in men whose cancer is detected clinically. The balance of potential benefits (the reduction of morbidity and mortality from prostate cancer) and harms (false-positive results, unnecessary biopsies, and possible complications) of early treatment of the types of cancers found by screening, however, remains uncertain. Therefore, the benefits of screening for early prostate cancer remain unknown. Ongoing screening trials, and trials of treatment versus "watchful waiting" for cancers detected by screening, may help clarify the benefits of early detection of prostate cancer.

- Despite the absence of firm evidence of effectiveness, some clinicians may opt to perform prostate cancer screening for other reasons. Given the uncertainties and controversy surrounding prostate cancer screening, clinicians should not order the PSA test without first discussing with the patient the potential but uncertain benefits and the possible harms of prostate cancer screening. Men should be informed of the gaps in the evidence, and they should be assisted in considering their personal preferences and risk profile before deciding whether to be tested.

■ If early detection improves health outcomes, the population most likely to benefit from screening will be men aged 50 to 70 who are at average risk, and men older than 45 who are at increased risk (African American men and men with a family history of a first-degree relative with prostate cancer).[1] Benefits may be smaller in Asian Americans, Hispanics, and other racial and ethnic groups that have a lower risk of prostate cancer. Older men and men with other significant medical problems who have a life expectancy of fewer than 10 years are unlikely to benefit from screening.[1]

■ PSA testing is more sensitive than DRE for the detection of prostate cancer. PSA screening with the conventional cut-point of 4.0 ng/ml detects a large majority of prostate cancers; however, a significant percentage of early prostate cancers (10% to 20%) will be missed by PSA testing alone.[2] Using a lower threshold to define an abnormal PSA detects more cancers at the cost of more false positives and more biopsies. The yield of screening in terms of cancer detected declines rapidly with repeated annual testing.[1] If screening were to reduce mortality, biennial PSA screening could yield as much benefit as annual screening.

References

1. Harris RP, Lohr KN. Screening for prostate cancer: an update of the evidence for the U.S. Preventive Services Task Force. *Ann Intern Med.* 2002; 137:917-929.

2. Harris RP, Lohr KN, Beck R, Fink K, Godley P, Bunton A. *Screening for Prostate Cancer.* Systematic Evidence Review No. 16 (Prepared by the Research Triangle Institute-University of North Carolina Evidence-based Practice Center under Contract No. 290-97-0011). Rockville, MD: Agency for Healthcare Research and Quality. December 2001. (Available on the AHRQ Web site at: www.ahrq.gov/clinic/serfiles.htm).

This USPSTF recommendation was first published in: *Ann Intern Med.* 2002;137:915-916.

Counseling to Prevent Skin Cancer

Summary of Recommendation

The U.S. Preventive Services Task Force (USPSTF) concludes that the evidence is insufficient to recommend for or against routine counseling by primary care clinicians to prevent skin cancer. *Rating: I Recommendation.*

Clinical Considerations

■ Using sunscreen has been shown to prevent squamous cell skin cancer. The evidence for the effect of sunscreen use in preventing melanoma, however, is mixed. Sunscreens that block both ultraviolet A (UV-A) and ultraviolet B (UV-B) light may be more effective in preventing squamous cell cancer and its precursors than those that block only UV-B light. However, people who use sunscreen alone could increase their risk for melanoma if they increase the time they spend in the sun.

■ UV exposure increases the risk for skin cancer among people with all skin types, but especially fair-skinned people. Those who sunburn readily and tan poorly, namely those with red or blond hair and fair skin that freckles or burns easily, are at highest risk for developing skin cancer and would benefit most from sun protection behaviors. The incidence of melanoma among whites is 20 times higher than it is among blacks; the incidence of melanoma among whites is about 4 times higher than it is among Hispanics.

- Observational studies indicate that intermittent or intense sun exposure is a greater risk factor for melanoma than chronic exposure. These studies support the hypothesis that preventing sunburn, especially in childhood, may reduce the lifetime risk for melanoma.

- Other measures for preventing skin cancer include avoiding direct exposure to midday sun (between the hours of 10:00 AM and 4:00 PM) to reduce exposure to ultraviolet (UV) rays and covering skin exposed to the sun (by wearing protective clothing such as broad-brimmed hats, long-sleeved shirts, long pants, and sunglasses).

- The effects of sunlamps and tanning beds on the risk for melanoma are unclear due to limited study design and conflicting results from retrospective studies.

- Only a single case-control study of skin self-examination has reported a lower risk for melanoma among patients who reported ever examining their skin over 5 years. Although results from this study suggest that skin self-examination may be effective in preventing skin cancer, these results are not definitive.

This USPSTF recommendation was first published by: Agency for Healthcare Research and Quality, Rockville, MD. October 2003. http://www.ahrq.gov/clinic/3rduspstf/ skcacoun/skcarr.htm.

Screening for Skin Cancer

Summary of Recommendation

The U.S. Preventive Services Task Force (USPSTF) concludes that the evidence is insufficient to recommend for or against routine screening for skin cancer using a total-body skin examination for the early detection of cutaneous melanoma, basal cell cancer, or squamous cell skin cancer. *Rating: I Recommendation.*

Clinical Considerations

- Benefits from screening are unproven, even in high-risk patients. Clinicians should be aware that fair-skinned men and women aged >65, patients with atypical moles, and those with >50 moles constitute known groups at substantially increased risk for melanoma.

- Clinicians should remain alert for skin lesions with malignant features noted in the context of physical examinations performed for other purposes. Asymmetry, border irregularity, color variability, diameter >6 mm ("A," "B," "C," "D"), or rapidly changing lesions are features associated with an increased risk of malignancy. Suspicious lesions should be biopsied.

■ The USPSTF did not examine the outcomes related to surveillance of patients with familial syndromes, such as familial atypical mole and melanoma (FAM-M) syndrome.

This USPSTF recommendation was first published in: *Am J Prev Med.* 2001;20(3S):44-46.

Screening for Testicular Cancer

Summary of Recommendation

The U.S. Preventive Services Task Force (USPSTF) recommends against routine screening for testicular cancer in asymptomatic adolescent and adult males. *Rating: D Recommendation.*

Clinical Considerations

■ The low incidence of testicular cancer and favorable outcomes in the absence of screening make it unlikely that clinical testicular examinations would provide important health benefits. Clinical examination by a physician and self-examination are the potential screening options for testicular cancer. However, little evidence is av accuracy, yield, or benefits of screening for testicular cancer

■ Although currently most testicular cancers are discovered by patients themselves or their partners, either unintentionally or by self-examination, there is no evidence that teaching young men how to examine themselves for testicular cancer would improve health outcomes, even among men at high risk, including men with a history of undescended testes or testicular atrophy.

■ Clinicians should be aware of testicular cancer as a possible diagnosis when young men present to them with suggestive signs and symptoms. There is some evidence that patients who present initially with symptoms of testicular cancer are frequently diagnosed as having epididymitis, testicular trauma, hydrocele, or other benign disorders. Efforts to promote prompt assessment and better evaluation of testicular problems may be more effective than widespread screening as a means of promoting early detection.

This USPSTF recommendation was first published by: Agency for Healthcare Research and Quality, Rockville, MD. February 2004. http://www.ahrq.gov/clinic/3rduspstf/testicular/testiculrs.htm.

Routine Vitamin Supplementation to Prevent Cancer and Cardiovascular Disease

Summary of Recommendations

The U.S. Preventive Services Task Force (USPSTF) concludes that the evidence is insufficient to recommend for or against the use of supplements of vitamins A, C, or E; multivitamins with folic acid; or antioxidant combinations for the prevention of cancer or cardiovascular disease. *Rating: I Recommendation.*

The USPSTF recommends against the use of beta-carotene supplements, either alone or in combination, for the prevention of cancer or cardiovascular disease. *Rating: D Recommendation.*

Clinical Considerations

■ The USPSTF did not review evidence regarding vitamin supplementation for patients with known or potential nutritional deficiencies, including pregnant and lactating women, children, the elderly, and people with chronic illnesses. Dietary supplements may be appropriate for people whose diet does not provide the recommended dietary intake of specific vitamins. Individuals may wish to consult a health care provider to discuss whether dietary supplements are appropriate.

■ With the exception of vitamins for which there is compelling evidence of net harm (e.g., beta-carotene supplementation in smokers), there is little reason to discourage people from taking vitamin supplements. Patients should be reminded that taking vitamins does not replace the need to eat a healthy diet. All patients should receive information about the benefits of a diet high in fruit and vegetables, as well as information on other foods and nutrients that should be emphasized or avoided in their diet (see 2002 USPSTF recommendation on counseling to promote a healthy diet, P. 125).

■ Patients who choose to take vitamins should be encouraged to adhere to the dosages recommended in the Dietary Reference Intakes (DRI) of the Institute of Medicine. Some vitamins, such as A and D, may be harmful in higher doses; therefore, doses greatly exceeding the Recommended Dietary Allowance (RDA) or Adequate Intake (AI) should be taken with care while considering whether potential harms outweigh potential benefits. Vitamins and minerals sold in the United States are classified as "dietary supplements," and there is a degree of quality control over content if they have a U.S. Pharmacopeia (USP) seal.[1] Nevertheless, imprecision in the content and concentration of ingredients could pose a theoretical risk not reflected in clinical trials using calibrated compounds.

- The adverse effects of beta-carotene on smokers have been observed primarily in those taking large supplemental doses. There is no evidence to suggest that beta-carotene is harmful to smokers at levels occurring naturally in foods.

- The USPSTF did not review evidence supporting folic acid supplementation among pregnant women to reduce neural tube defects. In 1996, the USPSTF recommended folic acid for all women who are planning, or capable of, pregnancy (see 1996 USPSTF chapter on screening for neural tube defects).[2]

- Clinicians and patients should discuss the possible need for vitamin supplementation when taking certain medications (e.g., folic acid supplementation for those patients taking methotrexate).

References

1. U.S. Pharmacopeia Dietary Supplement Verification Program. Available at: http://www.usp-dsvp.org. Accessed April 30, 2002.

2. Screening for Neural Tube Defects. U.S. Preventive Services Task Force. *Guide To Clinical Preventive Services.* 2nd ed. Washington, DC: Office of Disease Prevention and Health Promotion; 1996: 467-483. Available at: http://www.ahrq.gov/clinic/uspstf/uspsneur.htm. Accessed May 8, 2003.

This USPSTF recommendation was first published in: *Ann Intern Med.* 2003;139:51-55.

Heart and Vascular Diseases

Screening for Abdominal Aortic Aneurysm

Summary of Recommendations

The U.S. Preventive Services Task Force (USPSTF) recommends one-time screening for abdominal aortic aneurysm (AAA) by ultrasonography in men aged 65 to 75 who have ever smoked. *Rating: B Recommendation.*

The USPSTF makes no recommendation for or against screening for AAA in men aged 65 to 75 who have never smoked. *Rating: C Recommendation.*

The USPSTF recommends against routine screening for AAA in women. *Rating: D Recommendation.*

Clinical Considerations

- The major risk factors for abdominal aortic aneurysm (AAA) include age (being 65 or older), male sex, and a history of ever smoking (at least 100 cigarettes in a person's lifetime). A first-degree family history of AAA requiring surgical repair also elevates a man's risk for AAA; this may also be true for women but the evidence is less certain. There is only a modest association between risk factors for atherosclerotic disease and AAA.

■ Screening for AAA would most benefit those who have a reasonably high probability of having an AAA large enough, or that will become large enough, to benefit from surgery. In general, adults younger than age 65 and adults of any age who have never smoked are at low risk for AAA and are not likely to benefit from screening. Among men aged 65 to 74, an estimated 500 who have ever smoked—or 1,783 who have never smoked—would need to be screened to prevent 1 AAA-related death in the next 5 years. As always, clinicians must individualize recommendations depending on a patient's risk and likelihood of benefit. For example, some clinicians may choose to discuss screening with male nonsmokers nearing age 65 who have a strong first-degree family history of AAA that required surgery.

■ The potential benefit of screening for AAA among women aged 65 to 75 is low because of the small number of AAA-related deaths in this population. The majority of deaths from AAA rupture occur in women aged 80 or older. Because there are many competing health risks at this age, any benefit of screening for AAA would be minimal. Individualization of care, however, is still required. For example, a clinician may choose to discuss screening in the unusual circumstance in which a healthy female smoker in her early 70s has a first-degree family history for AAA that required surgery.

■ Operative mortality for open surgical repair of an AAA is 4 to 5 percent, and nearly one-third of patients undergoing this surgery have other important complications (e.g., cardiac and pulmonary). Additionally, men having this surgery are at increased risk for impotence.

■ Endovascular repair of AAAs (EVAR) is currently being used as an alternative to open surgical repair. Although recent studies have shown a short-term mortality and morbidity benefit of EVAR compared with open surgical repair, the long-term effectiveness of EVAR to reduce AAA rupture and mortality is unknown. The long-term harms of EVAR include late conversion to open repair and aneurysmal rupture. EVAR performed with older-generation devices is reported to have an annual rate of rupture of 1 percent and conversion to open surgical repair of 2 percent. The conversion to open surgical repair is associated with a peri-operative mortality of about 24 percent. The long-term harms of newer generation EVAR devices are yet to be reported.

■ For most men, 75 years may be considered an upper age limit for screening. Patients cannot benefit from screening and subsequent surgery unless they have a reasonable life expectancy. The increased presence of comorbidities for people aged 75 and older decreases the likelihood that they will benefit from screening.

■ Ultrasonography has a sensitivity of 95 percent and specificity of nearly 100 percent when performed in a setting with adequate quality assurance. The absence of quality assurance is likely to lower test accuracy. Abdominal palpation has poor accuracy and is not an adequate screening test.

■ One-time screening to detect an AAA using ultrasonography is sufficient. There is negligible health benefit in re-screening those who have normal aortic diameter on initial screening.

■ Open surgical repair for an AAA of at least 5.5 cm leads to an estimated 43-percent reduction in AAA-specific mortality in older men who undergo screening. However, there is no current evidence that screening reduces all-cause mortality in this population.

■ In men with intermediate-sized AAAs (4.0-5.4 cm), periodic surveillance offers comparable mortality benefit to routine elective surgery with the benefit of fewer operations. Although there is no evidence to support the effectiveness of any intervention in those with small AAAs (3.0-3.9 cm), there are expert opinion-based recommendations in favor of periodic repeat ultrasonography for these patients.

This USPSTF recommendation was first published in: *Ann Intern Med.* 2005;142:198-202.

Aspirin for the Primary Prevention of Cardiovascular Events

Summary of Recommendation

The U.S. Preventive Services Task Force (USPSTF) strongly recommends that clinicians discuss aspirin chemoprevention with adults who are at increased risk for coronary heart disease (CHD). Discussions with patients should address both the potential benefits and harms of aspirin therapy. *Rating: A Recommendation.*

Clinical Considerations

■ Decisions about aspirin therapy should take into account overall risk for coronary heart disease. Risk assessment should include asking about the presence and severity of the following risk factors: age, sex, diabetes, elevated total cholesterol levels, low levels of high-density lipoprotein (HDL) cholesterol, elevated blood pressure, family history (in younger adults), and smoking. Tools that incorporate specific information on multiple risk factors provide more accurate estimation of cardiovascular risk than categorizations based simply on counting the numbers of risk factors (http://www.intmed.mcw.edu/clincalc/heartrisk.html).[1]

■ Men older than 40 years, postmenopausal women, and younger people with risk factors for CHD (e.g., hypertension, diabetes, or smoking) are at increased risk for heart disease and may wish to consider aspirin therapy. Table 1 shows how estimates of the type and magnitude of benefits and harms associated with aspirin therapy vary with an individual's underlying risk for coronary heart disease. Although balance of benefits and harms is most favorable in high-risk people (5-year risk > 3%), some people at lower risk may consider the potential benefits of aspirin to be sufficient to outweigh the potential harms.

■ Discussions about aspirin therapy should focus on potential coronary heart disease benefits, such as prevention of myocardial infarction, and potential harms, such as gastrointestinal and intracranial bleeding. Discussions should take into account individual preferences and risk aversions concerning myocardial infarction, stroke, and gastrointestinal bleeding.

■ Although the optimal timing and frequency of discussions related to aspirin therapy are unknown, reasonable options include every 5 years in middle-aged and older people or when other cardiovascular risk factors are detected.

■ Most participants in the primary prevention trials of aspirin therapy have been men between 40 and 75 years of age. Current estimates of benefits and harms may not be as reliable for women and older men.

- Although older patients may derive greater benefits because they are at higher risk for CHD and stroke, their risk for bleeding may be higher.

- Uncontrolled hypertension may attenuate the benefits of aspirin in reducing CHD.

- The optimum dose of aspirin for chemoprevention is not known. Primary and secondary prevention trials have demonstrated benefits with a variety of regimens, including 75 mg per day, 100 mg per day, and 325 mg every other day. Doses of approximately 75 mg per day appear as effective as higher doses; whether doses below 75 mg per day are effective has not been established. Enteric-coated or buffered preparations do not clearly reduce adverse gastrointestinal effects of aspirin. Uncontrolled hypertension and concomitant use of other nonsteroidal anti-inflammatory agents or anticoagulants increase risk for serious bleeding.

Table 1. Estimates of Benefits and Harms of Asprin Therapy Given for 5 Years to 1,000 Individuals with Various Levels of Baseline Risk for Coronary Heart Disease*

Baseline risk for coronary heart disease over 5 years: 1%
Total mortality: No effect
CHD events**: 1-4 avoided
Hemorrhagic strokes***: 0-2 caused
Major gastrointestinal bleeding events****: 2-4 caused

Baseline risk for coronary heart disease over 5 years: 3%
Total mortality: No effect
CHD events**: 4-12 avoided
Hemorrhagic strokes***: 0-2 caused
Major gastrointestinal bleeding events****: 2-4 caused

Baseline risk for coronary heart disease over 5 years: 5%
Total mortality: No effect
CHD events**: 6-20 avoided
Hemorrhagic strokes***: 0-2 caused
Major gastrointestinal bleeding events****: 2-4 caused

* These estimates are based on a relative risk reduction of 28% for coronary heart disease events in aspirin-treated patients. They assume risk reductions do not vary significantly by age.

** Nonfatal acute myocardial infarction and fatal coronary heart disease. Five-year risks of 1%, 3% and 5% are equivalent to 10-year risks of 2%, 6%, and 10%, respectively.

*** Data from secondary prevention trials suggest that increases in hemorrhagic stroke may be offset by reduction in other types of stroke in patients at very high risk for cardiovascular disease (CVD) (greater than or equal to 10% 5-year risk).

**** Rates may be 2 to 3 times higher in people older than 70 years.

Reference

1. Wilson PW, D'Agostino RB, Levy D, Belanger AM, Sibershatz H, Kannel WB. Prediction of coronary heart disease using risk factor categories. *Circulation.* 1998;97(18):1837-1847.

2. Hayden M, Pignone M, Phillips C, Mulrow C. Aspirin for the primary prevention of cardiovascular events: A summary of the evidence for the U.S. Preventive Services Task Force. *Annals of Internal Medicine.* 2002;136:161-172.

This USPSTF recommendation was first published in: *Ann Intern Med.* 2002;136(2):157-160.

Screening for Coronary Heart Disease

Summary of Recommendations

The U.S. Preventive Services Task Force (USPSTF) recommends against routine screening with resting electrocardiography (ECG), exercise treadmill test (ETT), or electron-beam computerized tomography (EBCT) scanning for coronary calcium for either the presence of severe coronary artery stenosis (CAS) or the prediction of coronary heart disease (CHD) events in adults at low risk for CHD events. *Rating: D Recommendation.*

The USPSTF found insufficient evidence to recommend for or against routine screening with ECG, ETT, or EBCT scanning for coronary calcium for either the presence of severe CAS or the prediction of CHD events in adults at increased risk for CHD events. *Rating: I Recommendation.*

Clinical Considerations

■ Several factors are associated with a higher risk for CHD events (the major ones are nonfatal myocardial infarction and coronary death), including older age, male gender, high blood pressure, smoking, abnormal lipid levels, diabetes, obesity, and sedentary lifestyle. A person's risk for CHD events can be estimated based on the presence of these factors. Calculators are available to ascertain a person's risk for having a CHD event; for example, a calculator to estimate a person's risk for a CHD event in the next 10 years can be accessed at http://hin.nhlbi.nih.gov/atpiii/calculator.asp?usertype=prof. Although the exact risk factors that constitute each of these categories (low or increased risk) have not been established, younger adults (ie, men < 50 years and women < 60 years) who have no other risk factors for CHD (< 5%-10% 10-year risk) are considered to be at low risk. Older adults, or younger adults with 1 or more risk factors (> 15% -20% 10-year risk), are considered to be at increased risk.

■ Screening with ECG, ETT, and EBCT could potentially reduce CHD events in 2 ways: either by detecting people at high risk for CHD events who could benefit from more aggressive risk factor modification, or by detecting people with existing severe CAS whose life could be prolonged by coronary artery bypass grafting (CABG) surgery. However, the evidence is inadequate to determine the extent to which people detected through screening in either situation would benefit from either type of intervention.

■ The consequences of false-positive tests may potentially outweigh the benefits of screening. False-positive tests are common among asymptomatic adults, especially women, and may lead to unnecessary diagnostic testing, over-treatment, and labeling.

■ Because the sensitivity of these tests is limited, screening could also result in false-negative results. A negative test does not rule out the presence of severe CAS or a future CHD event.

■ For people in certain occupations, such as pilots and heavy equipment operators (for whom sudden incapacitation or sudden death may endanger the safety of others), considerations other than the health benefit to the individual patient may influence the decision to screen for CHD.

■ Although some exercise programs initially screen asymptomatic participants with ETT, there is not enough evidence to determine the balance of benefits and harms of this practice.

This USPSTF recommendation was first published in: *Ann Intern Med.* 2004;140:569-572.

Screening for High Blood Pressure

Summary of Recommendations

The U.S. Preventive Services Task Force (USPSTF) strongly recommends that clinicians screen adults aged 18 and older for high blood pressure. *Rating: A Recommendation.*

The USPSTF concludes that the evidence is insufficient to recommend for or against routine screening for high blood pressure in children and adolescents to reduce the risk of cardiovascular disease. *Rating: I Recommendation.*

Clinical Considerations

■ Office measurement of blood pressure is most commonly done with a sphygmomanometer. High blood pressure (hypertension) is usually defined in adults as a systolic blood pressure (SBP) of 140 mm Hg or higher, or a diastolic blood pressure (DBP) of 90 mm Hg or higher. Due to variability in individual blood pressure measurements (occurring as a result of instrument, observer, and patient factors), it is recommended that hypertension be diagnosed only after 2 or more elevated readings are obtained on at least 2 visits over a period of 1 to several weeks.

■ There are some data to suggest that ambulatory blood pressure measurement (that provides a measure of the average blood pressure over 24 hours) may be a better predictor of clinical cardiovascular outcome than clinic-based approaches; however, ambulatory blood pressure measurement is subject to many of the same errors as office blood pressure measurement.

■ The relationship between SBP and DBP and cardiovascular risk is continuous and graded. The actual level of blood pressure elevation should not be the sole factor in determining treatment. Clinicians should consider the patient's overall cardiovascular risk profile, including smoking, diabetes, abnormal blood lipids, age, sex, sedentary lifestyle, and obesity, in making treatment decisions.

■ Hypertension in children has been defined as blood pressure above the 95th percentile for age, sex, and height. Up to 28% of children have secondary hypertension, ie, high blood pressure due to causes such as coarctation of the aorta, renal parenchymal disease, renal artery stenosis, and other congenital malformations. On the basis of expert opinion, several organizations, including the American Academy of Pediatrics (AAP), American Heart Association (AHA), and American Medical Association (AMA), recommend routine screening of asymptomatic adolescents and children during preventive care visits, based on the potential for identifying treatable causes of secondary hypertension, such as coarctation of aorta. However, there are limited data on the benefits or risks of screening and treating such underlying causes of hypertension in children. The decision to screen children and adolescents for hypertension remains a matter of clinical judgment.

■ Evidence is lacking to recommend an optimal interval for screening adults for high blood pressure. The sixth report of the Joint National Committee on Prevention, Detection, Evaluation, and Treatment of High Blood Pressure (JNC 6) recommends screening every 2 years for persons with SBP and DBP below 130 mm Hg and 85 mm Hg, respectively, and more frequent intervals for screening those with blood pressure at higher levels.

■ A variety of pharmacological agents are available to treat high blood pressure. JNC 6 guidelines for treatment of high blood pressure can be accessed at www.nhlbi.nih.gov/guidelines/hypertension/jncintro .htm. The JNC 6-recommended goal of treatment is to achieve and maintain SBP below 140 mm Hg and DBP below 90 mm Hg, and lower if tolerated. Evidence indicates that reducing DBP to below 80 mm Hg appears to be beneficial for patients with hypertension and diabetes. In considering the effectiveness of treatment for hypertension, it must be noted that a given treatment's ability to lower blood pressure may not correspond directly to its ability to reduce cardiovascular events.

■ Nonpharmacological therapies, such as reducing dietary sodium intake, potassium supplementation, increased physical activity, weight loss, stress management, and reducing alcohol intake, are associated with a reduction in blood pressure, but their impact on cardiovascular outcomes has not been studied. For those who consume large amounts of alcohol (more than 20 drinks in a week), studies have shown that reduced drinking decreases blood pressure. There is insufficient evidence to recommend single or multiple interventions or to guide the clinician in selecting among nonpharmacological therapies.

This USPSTF recommendation was first published by: Agency for Healthcare Research and Quality, Rockville, MD. July 2003. http://www.ahrq.gov/clinic/uspstf/uspshype.htm.

Screening for Lipid Disorders in Adults

Summary of Recommendations

The U.S. Preventive Services Task Force (USPSTF) strongly recommends that clinicians routinely screen men aged 35 years and older and women aged 45 years and older for lipid disorders and treat abnormal lipids in people who are at increased risk for coronary heart disease. *Rating: A Recommendation.*

The USPSTF recommends that clinicians routinely screen younger adults (men aged 20 to 35 years and women aged 20 to 45 years) for lipid disorders if they have other risk factors for coronary heart disease. (See Clinical Considerations for a discussion of risk factors.) *Rating: B Recommendation.*

The USPSTF makes no recommendation for or against routine screening for lipid disorders in younger adults (men aged 20 to 35 years or women aged 20 to 45 years) in the absence of known risk factors for coronary heart disease. *Rating: C Recommendation.*

The USPSTF recommends that screening for lipid disorders include measurement of total cholesterol (TC) and high-density lipoprotein cholesterol (HDL-C). *Rating: B Recommendation.*

The USPSTF concludes that the evidence is insufficient to recommend for or against triglyceride measurement as a part of routine screening for lipid disorders. *Rating: I Recommendation.*

Clinical Considerations

■ TC and HDL-C can be measured on nonfasting or fasting samples.

■ Abnormal results should be confirmed by a repeated sample on a separate occasion, and the average of both results should be used for risk assessment. Although measuring both TC and HDL-C is more sensitive and specific for assessing coronary heart disease risk, TC alone is an acceptable screening test if available laboratory services cannot provide reliable measurements of HDL. In conjunction with HDL-C, low-density lipoprotein cholesterol (LDL-C) and TC provide comparable information, but measuring LDL-C requires a fasting sample and is more expensive. In patients with elevated risk on screening results, lipoprotein analysis, including fasting triglycerides, may provide information that is useful in choosing optimal treatments.

■ Screening is recommended for men aged 20 to 35 years and for women aged 20 to 45 years in the presence of any of the following:

■ Diabetes.

■ A family history of cardiovascular disease before age 50 years in male relatives or age 60 years in female relatives.

■ A family history suggestive of familial hyperlipidemia.

■ Multiple coronary heart disease risk factors (e.g., tobacco use, hypertension).

■ The optimal interval for screening is uncertain. On the basis of other guidelines and expert opinion, reasonable options include every 5 years, shorter intervals for people who have lipid levels close to those warranting therapy, and longer intervals for low-risk people who have had low or repeatedly normal lipid levels.

■ An age to stop screening is not established. Screening may be appropriate in older people who have never been screened, but repeated screening is less important in older people because lipid levels are less likely to increase after age 65 years.

■ Treatment decisions should take into account overall risk of heart disease rather than lipid levels alone. Overall risk assessment should include the presence and severity of the following risk factors: age, gender, diabetes, elevated blood pressure, family history (in younger adults), and smoking. Tools that incorporate specific information on multiple risk factors provide more accurate estimation of cardiovascular risk than categorizations based on counting the numbers of risk factors.[1,2]

■ Treatment choices should take into account costs and patient preferences. Drug therapy is usually more effective than diet alone, but choice of treatment should consider overall risk, costs of treatment, and patient preferences. Guidelines for treating high cholesterol are available from the National Cholesterol Education Program of the National Institutes of Health.[3] Although diet therapy is an appropriate initial therapy for most patients, a minority achieve substantial reductions in lipid levels

73

from diet alone; drugs are frequently needed to achieve therapeutic goals, especially for high-risk people. Lipid-lowering treatments should be accompanied by interventions addressing all modifiable risk factors for heart disease, including smoking cessation, treatment of blood pressure, diabetes, and obesity, as well as promotion of a healthy diet and regular physical activity. Long-term adherence to therapies should be emphasized.

■ All patients, regardless of lipid levels, should be offered counseling about the benefits of a diet low in saturated fat and high in fruits and vegetables, regular physical activity, avoiding tobacco use, and maintaining a healthy weight.

References

1. Wilson PW, D'Agostino RB, Levy D, Belanger AM, Silbershatz H, Kannel WB. Prediction of coronary heart disease using risk factor categories. *Circulation.*1998, 97:1837-1847.

2. Jackson R. Updated New Zealand cardiovascular disease risk-benefit prediction guide. *BMJ.* 2000;320:709-710. Also available at: www.bmj.com/cgi/content/full/320/7236/709.

3. Summary of the second report of the National Cholesterol Education Program (NCEP) Expert Panel on the Detection, Evaluation, and Treatment of High Blood Cholesterol in Adults (Adult Treatment Panel II). *JAMA.* 1993;269:3015-3023.

This USPSTF recommendation was first published in: *Am J Prev Med.* 2001;20(3S):73-76.

Screening for Peripheral Arterial Disease

Summary of Recommendation

The U.S. Preventive Services Task Force (USPSTF) recommends against routine screening for peripheral arterial disease (PAD). *Rating: D Recommendation.*

Clinical Considerations

■ The ankle brachial index, a ratio of Doppler-recorded systolic pressures in the lower and upper extremities, is a simple and accurate noninvasive test for the screening and diagnosis of PAD. The ankle brachial index has demonstrated better accuracy than other methods of screening, including history-taking, questionnaires, and palpation of peripheral pulses. An ankle-brachial index value of less than 0.90 (95% sensitive and specific for angiographic PAD) is strongly associated with limitations in lower extremity functioning and physical activity tolerance.

■ Smoking cessation and lipid-lowering agents improve claudication symptoms and lower extremity functioning among patients with symptomatic PAD. Smoking cessation and physical activity training also increase maximal walking distance among men with early PAD. Counseling for smoking cessation, however, should be offered to all patients who smoke, regardless of the presence of PAD. Similarly, physically inactive patients should be counseled to increase their physical activity, regardless of the presence of PAD.

This USPSTF recommendation was first published by: Agency for Healthcare Research and Quality, Rockville, MD. August 2005. http://www.ahrq.gov/clinic/uspstf05/ pad/padrs.htm.

Infectious Diseases

Screening for Asymptomatic Bacteriuria

Summary of Recommendations

The U.S. Preventive Services Task Force (USPSTF) strongly recommends that all pregnant women be screened for asymptomatic bacteriuria using urine culture at 12-16 weeks' gestation. *Rating: A Recommendation.*

The USPSTF recommends against the routine screening of men and nonpregnant women for asymptomatic bacteriuria. *Rating: D Recommendation.*

Clinical Considerations

■ The screening tests used commonly in the primary care setting (dipstick analysis and direct microscopy) have poor positive and negative predictive value for detecting bacteriuria in asymptomatic persons. Urine culture is the gold standard for detecting asymptomatic bacteriuria but is expensive for routine screening in populations with a low prevalence of this condition. Results from one study done with a new enzymatic urine-screening test (Uriscreen™) showed that the test has a sensitivity of 100% and a specificity of 81%.

■ Good evidence exists that screening pregnant women for asymptomatic bacteriuria with urine culture (rather than urinalysis) significantly reduces symptomatic urinary tract infections, low birth weight, and preterm delivery. A specimen obtained at 12-16 weeks' gestation will detect approximately 80% of patients with asymptomatic bacteriuria. The optimal frequency of subsequent urine testing during pregnancy is uncertain.

■ Good evidence exists that screening individuals other than pregnant women for asymptomatic bacteriuria does not significantly improve clinical outcomes. Results from a study of women with diabetes who were treated for asymptomatic bacteriuria demonstrated no reduction in complications.[1] Although there were short-term results in clearing bacteriuria with antimicrobial therapy, there was no decrease in the number of symptomatic episodes or hospitalizations over the long term. Furthermore, the high rate of recurrence of bacteriuria in those who were screened and treated resulted in a marked increase in the use of antimicrobial agents.

Reference

1. Harding GKM, Zhanel GG, Nicolle LE, Cheang M. Antimicrobial treatment in diabetic women with asymptomatic bacteriuria. *N Engl J Med.* 2002; 347(20):1576-1583.

This USPSTF recommendation was first published by: Agency for Healthcare Research and Quality, Rockville, MD. February 2004. http://www.ahrq.gov/clinic/3rduspstf/ asymbac/asymbacrs.htm.

Screening for Chlamydial Infection

Summary of Recommendations

The U.S. Preventive Services Task Force (USPSTF) strongly recommends that clinicians routinely screen all sexually active women aged 25 years and younger, and other asymptomatic women at increased risk for infection, for chlamydial infection (see Clinical Considerations for discussion of risk factors). *Rating: A Recommendation.*

The USPSTF makes no recommendation for or against routinely screening asymptomatic low-risk women in the general population for chlamydial infection. *Rating: C Recommendation.*

The USPSTF recommends that clinicians routinely screen all asymptomatic pregnant women aged 25 years and younger and others at increased risk for chlamydial infection (see Clinical Considerations for discussion of risk factors in pregnancy). *Rating: B Recommendation.*

The USPSTF makes no recommendation for or against routine screening of asymptomatic, low-risk pregnant women aged 26 years and older for chlamydial infection. *Rating: C Recommendation.*

The USPSTF concludes that the evidence is insufficient to recommend for or against routinely screening asymptomatic men for chlamydial infection. *Rating: I Recommendation.*

Clinical Considerations

■ Women and adolescents through age 20 years are at highest risk for chlamydial infection, but most reported data indicate that infection is prevalent among women aged 20-25.

■ Age is the most important risk marker. Other patient characteristics associated with a higher prevalence of infection include being unmarried, African-American race, having a prior history of sexually transmitted disease (STD), having new or multiple sexual partners, having cervical ectopy, and using barrier contraceptives inconsistently. Individual risk depends on the number of risk markers and local prevalence of the disease. Specific risk-based screening protocols need to be tested at the local level.

■ Clinicians should consider the characteristics of the communities they serve in determining appropriate screening strategies for their patient population.

■ More targeted screening may be indicated in specific settings as better prevalence data become available. Prevalence of chlamydial infection varies widely among communities and patient populations. Knowledge of the patient population is the best guide to developing a screening strategy. Local public health authorities can be a source of valuable information.

■ The optimal interval for screening is uncertain. For women with a previous negative screening test, the interval for rescreening should take into account changes in sexual partners. If there is evidence that a woman is at low risk for infection (e.g., in a mutually monogamous relationship with a previous history of negative screening tests for chlamydial infection), it may not be necessary to screen frequently. Rescreening at 6 to 12 months may be appropriate for previously infected women because of high rates of reinfection.

■ The optimal timing of screening in pregnancy is also uncertain. Screening early in pregnancy provides greater opportunities to improve pregnancy outcomes, including low birth weight and premature delivery; however, screening in the third trimester may be more effective at preventing transmission of chlamydial infection to the infant during birth. The incremental benefit of repeated screening is unknown.

■ Screening high-risk young men is a clinical option. Until the advent of urine-based screening tests, routine screening of men was rarely performed. As a result, very little evidence regarding the efficacy of screening in men in reducing infection among women exists. Trials are underway to assess the effectiveness of screening asymptomatic men.

■ The choice of specific screening technique is left to clinical judgment. Choice of test will depend on issues of cost, convenience, and feasibility, which may vary in different settings. Although specificity is high with most approved tests, false-positive results can occur with all non-culture tests and rarely with culture tests. Subsequent to initial release of this recommendation, the Centers for Disease Control and Prevention (CDC) released laboratory guidelines that outline the advantages and disadvantages of available tests. These guidelines are available at http://www.cdc.gov/STD/ LabGuidelines.

■ Partners of infected individuals should be tested and treated if infected or treated presumptively.

■ Clinicians should remain alert for findings suggestive of chlamydial infection during pelvic examination of asymptomatic women (e.g., discharge, cervical erythema, and cervical friability).

■ Clinicians should be sensitive to the potential effect of diagnosing a sexually transmitted disease on a couple. To prevent false-positive results, confirmatory testing may be appropriate in settings with low population prevalence.

This USPSTF recommendation was first published in: *Am J Prev Med.* 2001;20(3S):90-94.

Screening for Genital Herpes

Summary of Recommendations

The U.S. Preventive Services Task Force (USPSTF) recommends against routine serological screening for herpes simplex virus (HSV) in asymptomatic pregnant women at any time during pregnancy to prevent neonatal HSV infection. *Rating: D Recommendation.*

The USPSTF recommends against routine serological screening for HSV in asymptomatic adolescents and adults. *Rating: D Recommendation.*

Clinical Considerations

■ Serological screening tests for genital herpes can detect prior infection with HSV in asymptomatic persons, and new type-specific serological tests can differentiate between HSV-1 and HSV-2 exposure (these tests cannot differentiate between oral vs genital herpes exposure); however, given the natural history of genital herpes, there is limited evidence to guide clinical intervention in those asymptomatic persons who have positive serological test results. False-positive test results may lead to labeling and psychological stress without any potential benefit to patients. Negative test results (both false-negative and true-negative results) may provide false reassurance to continue high-risk sexual behaviors.

■ There is new, good-quality evidence demonstrating that systemic antiviral therapy effectively reduces viral shedding and recurrences of genital herpes in

83

adolescents and adults with a history of recurrent genital herpes. There are multiple efficacious regimens that may be used to prevent the recurrence of clinical genital herpes.

■ The USPSTF did not examine the evidence for the effectiveness of counseling to avoid high-risk sexual behavior in persons with a history of genital herpes to prevent transmission to discordant partners, or for the primary prevention of genital herpes in persons not infected with HSV. There are known health benefits of avoiding high-risk sexual behavior, including prevention of sexually transmitted infections (STIs) and HIV infection.

■ Primary HSV infection during pregnancy presents the greatest risk for transmitting infection to the newborn. The fact that women with primary HSV infection are initially seronegative limits the usefulness of screening with antibody tests. The USPSTF did not find any studies testing the use of antibody screening to find and treat seronegative pregnant women (i.e., those at risk for primary HSV infection) prophylactically. However, the number of seronegative pregnant women one would need to treat to theoretically avoid one primary infection would be very high, making the potential benefit small. At the same time, the potential harm to many low-risk women and fetuses from the side effects of antiviral therapy may be great.

■ There is fair evidence that antiviral therapy in late pregnancy can reduce HSV recurrence and viral shedding at delivery in women with recurrent HSV infection; however, there is currently no evidence that antiviral use in women with a history of HSV leads to reduced neonatal infection. Likewise, there is limited information on the benefits of screening women in labor for signs of active genital HSV lesions, and for the performance of cesarean delivery on those with lesions.

This USPSTF recommendation was first published by: Agency for Healthcare Research and Quality. Rockville, MD, March 2005. http://www.ahrq.gov/clinic/uspstf05/herpes/herpesrs.htm.

Screening for Gonorrhea

Summary of Recommendations

The U.S. Preventive Services Task Force (USPSTF) recommends that clinicians screen all sexually active women, including those who are pregnant, for gonorrhea infection if they are at increased risk for infection (that is, if they are young or have other individual or population risk factors; see Clinical Considerations for further discussion of risk factors). *Rating: B Recommendation.*

The USPSTF found insufficient evidence to recommend for or against routine screening for gonorrhea infection in men at increased risk for infection (see Clinical Considerations for discussion of risk factors). *Rating: I Recommendation.*

The USPSTF recommends against routine screening for gonorrhea infection in men and women who are at low risk for infection (see Clinical Considerations for discussion of risk factors). *Rating: D Recommendation.*

The USPSTF found insufficient evidence to recommend for or against routine screening for gonorrhea infection in pregnant women who are not at increased risk for infection (see Clinical Considerations for discussion of risk factors). *Rating: I Recommendation.*

The USPSTF strongly recommends prophylactic ocular topical medication for all newborns against gonococcal ophthalmia neonatorum. *Rating: A Recommendation.*

Clinical Considerations

■ Women and men under the age of 25—including sexually active adolescents—are at highest risk for genital gonorrhea infection. Risk factors for gonorrhea include a history of previous gonorrhea infection, other sexually transmitted infections, new or multiple sexual partners, inconsistent condom use, sex work, and drug use. Risk factors for pregnant women are the same as for non-pregnant women. Prevalence of gonorrhea infection varies widely among communities and patient populations. African Americans and men who have sex with men have a higher prevalence of infection than the general population in many communities and settings.

■ Individual risk depends on the local epidemiology of disease. Local public health authorities provide guidance to clinicians to help identify populations who are at increased risk in their communities. In communities with a high prevalence of gonorrhea, broader screening of sexually active young people may be warranted, especially in settings serving individuals who are at increased risk. Additionally, clinicians may want to consider other population-based risk factors, including residence in urban communities and communities with high rates of poverty, when making screening decisions. Low community prevalence of gonorrhea infection may justify more targeted screening.

■ Screening is recommended at the first prenatal visit for pregnant women who are in a high risk group for gonorrhea infection. For pregnant patients who are at continued risk, and for those who acquire a new risk factor, a second screening should be conducted during the third trimester. The optimal interval for screening in the non-pregnant population is not known.

■ Vaginal culture remains an accurate screening test when transport conditions are suitable. Newer screening tests, including nucleic acid amplification tests and nucleic acid hybridization tests, have demonstrated improved sensitivity and comparable specificity when compared with cervical culture. Some newer tests can be used with urine and vaginal swabs, which enables screening when a pelvic examination is not performed.

■ Appropriate treatment of gonorrhea infection and administration of prophylactic medication to newborns have been outlined by the Centers for Disease Control and Prevention (CDC) (http://www.cdc.gov/std/treatment/42002TG.htm# Gonococcal). Genital infection in men and women may be treated with a third generation cephalosporin or fluoroquinolone, and pregnant women may be treated with third generation cephalosporins. Because of emerging fluoroquinolone resistance, the CDC issued new treatment guidelines in 2004 recommending that men who have sex with men and those who acquired an infection in California, Hawaii, or Asia not be treated with fluoroquinolone antibiotics. If clinicians have not concurrently screened for chlamydial infection, the CDC recommends presumptive treatment for chlamydia at the time of treatment for gonorrhea. In order to prevent recurrent transmission, partners of infected individuals should be tested and treated if infected, or treated presumptively.

■ Gonorrhea is a nationally reportable condition. More complete reporting of gonorrhea cases to public health authorities will permit more accurate estimations of gonorrhea prevalence. Improved information will allow clinicians to screen for gonorrhea in ways that improve the balance between benefits and harms for their patients.

■ Research priorities for gonorrhea screening include greater understanding of the benefits of screening men at increased risk, especially men who have sex with men, and the role of reporting on gonorrhea rates and testing priorities.

This USPSTF recommendation was first published in: *Ann Fam Med.* 2005;3:263-267.

Screening for Hepatitis B Virus Infection

Summary of Recommendations

The U.S. Preventive Services Task Force (USPSTF) strongly recommends screening for hepatitis B virus (HBV) infection in pregnant women at their first prenatal visit. *Rating: A Recommendation.*

The USPSTF recommends against routinely screening the general asymptomatic population for chronic hepatitis B virus infection. *Rating: D Recommendation.*

Clinical Considerations

- Routine hepatitis vaccination has had significant impact in reducing the number of new HBV infections per year, with the greatest decline among children and adolescents. Programs that vaccinate health care workers also reduce the transmission of HBV infection.

- Most people who become infected as adults or older children recover fully from HBV infection and develop protective immunity to the virus.

- The main risk factors for HBV infection in the United States include diagnosis with a sexually transmitted disease, intravenous drug use, sexual contact with multiple partners, male homosexual activity, and household contacts of chronically infected persons. However, screening strategies to identify individuals at high risk have poor predictive value, since 30% to 40% of infected individuals do not have any easily identifiable risk factors.

■ Important predictors of progressive HBV infection include longer duration of infection and the presence of comorbid conditions such as alcohol abuse, HIV, or other chronic liver disease. Individuals with HBV infection identified through screening may benefit from interventions designed to reduce liver injury from other causes, such as counseling to avoid alcohol abuse and immunization against hepatitis A. However, there is limited evidence on the effectiveness of these interventions.

This USPSTF recommendation was first published by: Agency for Healthcare Research and Quality, Rockville, MD. February 2004. http://www.ahrq.gov/clinic/ 3rduspstf/hepbscr/hepbrs.htm.

Screening for Hepatitis C in Adults

Summary of Recommendations

The U.S. Preventive Services Task Force (USPSTF) recommends against routine screening for hepatitis C virus (HCV) infection in asymptomatic adults who are not at increased risk (general population) for infection. *Rating: D Recommendation.*

The USPSTF found insufficient evidence to recommend for or against routine screening for HCV infection in adults at high risk for infection. *Rating: I Recommendation.*

Clinical Considerations

■ Established risk factors for HCV infection include current or past intravenous drug use, transfusion before 1990, dialysis, and being a child of an HCV-infected mother. Surrogate markers, such as high-risk sexual behavior (particularly sex with someone infected with HCV) and the use of illegal drugs, such as cocaine or marijuana, have also been associated with increased risk for HCV infection. The proportion of people who received blood or blood product transfusions before 1990 will continue to decline, and HCV infection will be associated mainly with intravenous drug use and, to some extent, unsafe sexual behaviors.

■ Initial testing for HCV infection is typically done by enzyme immunoassay (EIA). In a population with a low prevalence of HCV infection (e.g., 2%), approximately 59% of all positive tests using the third-generation EIA test with 97% specificity would be false positive. As a result, confirmatory testing is recommended with the strip recombinant immunoblot assay (third-generation RIBA).

■ Important predictors of progressive HCV infection include older age at acquisition; longer duration of infection; and presence of comorbid conditions, such as alcohol misuse, HIV infection, or other chronic liver disease. Asymptomatic individuals with HCV infection identified through screening may benefit from interventions designed to reduce liver injury from other causes, such as counseling to avoid alcohol misuse and immunization against hepatitis A and hepatitis B. However, there is limited evidence of the effectiveness of these interventions.

This USPSTF recommendation was first published in: *Ann Intern Med.* 2004;140(6):462-464.

Screening for HIV

Summary of Recommendations

The U.S. Preventive Services Task Force (USPSTF) strongly recommends that clinicians screen for human immunodeficiency virus (HIV) all adolescents and adults at increased risk for HIV infection. *Rating: A Recommendation.*

The USPSTF makes no recommendation for or against routinely screening for HIV adolescents and adults who are not at increased risk for HIV infection. *Rating: C Recommendation.*

The USPSTF recommends that clinicians screen all pregnant women for HIV. *Rating: A Recommendation.*

Clinical Considerations

- A person is considered at increased risk for HIV infection (and thus should be offered HIV testing) if he or she reports 1 or more individual risk factors or receives health care in a high-prevalence or high-risk clinical setting.

- Individual risk for HIV infection is assessed through a careful patient history. Those at increased risk (as determined by prevalence rates) include: men who have had sex with men after 1975; men and women having unprotected sex with multiple partners; past or present injection drug users; men and women who exchange sex for money or drugs or have sex partners who do; individuals whose past or present sex partners were HIV-infected, bisexual, or injection drug users; persons being treated for sexually transmitted diseases (STDs); and persons with a history of blood transfusion between 1978 and 1985. Persons who request an HIV test despite reporting no individual risk factors may also be considered at increased risk, since this group is likely to include individuals not willing to disclose high risk behaviors.

■ There is good evidence of increased yield from routine HIV screening of persons who report no individual risk factors but are seen in high-risk or high-prevalence clinical settings. High-risk settings include STD clinics, correctional facilities, homeless shelters, tuberculosis clinics, clinics serving men who have sex with men, and adolescent health clinics with a high prevalence of STDs. High-prevalence settings are defined by the Centers for Disease Control and Prevention (CDC) as those known to have a 1% or greater prevalence of infection among the patient population being served. Where possible, clinicians should consider the prevalence of HIV infection or the risk characteristics of the population they serve in determining an appropriate screening strategy. Data are currently lacking to guide clinical decisions about the optimal frequency of HIV screening.

■ Current evidence supports the benefit of identifying and treating asymptomatic individuals in immunologically advanced stages of HIV disease (CD4 cell counts < 200 cells/mm3) with highly active antiretroviral therapy (HAART). Appropriate prophylaxis and immunization against certain opportunistic infections have also been shown to be effective interventions for these individuals. Use of HAART can be considered for asymptomatic individuals who are in an earlier stage of disease but at high risk for disease progression (CD4 cell count < 350 cells/mm3 or viral load > 100,000 copies/mL), although definitive evidence of a significant benefit of starting HAART at these counts is currently lacking.

■ The standard test for diagnosing HIV infection, the repeatedly reactive enzyme immunoassay followed by confirmatory western blot or immunofluorescent assay, is highly accurate (sensitivity and specificity > 99%). Rapid HIV antibody testing is also highly accurate; can be performed in 10 to 30 minutes; and, when offered at the point of care, is useful for screening high risk patients who do not receive regular medical care (e.g., those seen in emergency departments), as well as women with unknown HIV status who present in active labor.

■ Early identification of maternal HIV seropositivity allows early antiretroviral treatment to prevent mother-to-child transmission, allows providers to avoid obstetric practices that may increase the risk for transmission, and allows an opportunity to counsel the mother against breastfeeding (also known to increase the risk for transmission). There is evidence that the adoption of "opt-out" strategies to screen pregnant women (who are informed that an HIV test will be conducted as a standard part of prenatal care unless they decline it) has resulted in higher testing rates. However, ethical and legal concerns of not obtaining specific informed consent for an HIV test using the "opt-out" strategy have been raised. While dramatic reductions in HIV transmission to neonates have been noted as a result of early prenatal detection and treatment, the extent to which detection of HIV infection and intervention during pregnancy may improve long-term maternal outcomes is unclear.

This USPSTF recommendation was first published in: *Ann Intern Med.* 2005;143:32-37.

Screening for Syphilis Infection

Summary of Recommendations

The U.S. Preventive Services Task Force (USPSTF) strongly recommends that clinicians screen persons at increased risk for syphilis infection. *Rating: A Recommendation.*

The USPSTF strongly recommends that clinicians screen all pregnant women for syphilis infection. *Rating: A Recommendation.*

The USPSTF recommends against routine screening of asymptomatic persons who are not at increased risk for syphilis infection. *Rating: D Recommendation.*

Clinical Considerations

■ Populations at increased risk for syphilis infection (as determined by incident rates) include men who have sex with men and engage in high-risk sexual behavior, commercial sex workers, persons who exchange sex for drugs, and those in adult correctional facilities. There is no evidence to support an optimal screening frequency in this population. Clinicians should consider the characteristics of the communities they serve in determining appropriate screening strategies. Prevalence of syphilis infection varies widely among communities and patient populations. For example, the prevalence of syphilis infection differs by region (the prevalence of infection is higher in the southern U.S. and in some metropolitan areas than it is in the U.S. as a whole) and by ethnicity (the prevalence of syphilis infection is higher in Hispanic and African American populations than it is in the white population).

■ Persons diagnosed with other sexually transmitted diseases (STDs) (ie, chlamydia, gonorrhea, genital herpes simplex, human papilloma virus, and HIV) may be more likely than others to engage in high-risk behavior, placing them at increased risk for syphilis; however, there is no evidence that supports the routine screening of individuals diagnosed with other STDs for syphilis infection. Clinicians should use clinical judgment to individualize screening for syphilis infection based on local prevalence and other risk factors (see above).

■ Nontreponemal tests commonly used for initial screening are the Venereal Disease Research Laboratory (VDRL) or Rapid Plasma Reagin (RPR), followed by a confirmatory fluorescent treponemal antibody absorbed (FTA-ABS) or T. pallidum particle agglutination (TP-PA). The optimal screening interval in average- and high-risk persons has not been determined.

■ All pregnant women should be tested at their first prenatal visit. For women in high-risk groups, repeat serologic testing may be necessary in the third trimester and at delivery. Follow-up serologic tests should be obtained to document decline initially after treatment. These follow-up tests should be performed using the same nontreponemal test initially used to document infections (e.g., VDRL or RPR) to ensure comparability.

This USPSTF recommendation was first published in: *Ann Fam Med.* 2004;2(4):362-365.

Injury and Violence

Screening for Family and Intimate Partner Violence

Summary of Recommendation

The U.S. Preventive Services Task Force (USPSTF) found insufficient evidence to recommend for or against routine screening of parents or guardians for the physical abuse or neglect of children, of women for intimate partner violence, or of older adults or their caregivers for elder abuse. *Rating: I Recommendation.*

Clinical Considerations

■ The USPSTF did not review the evidence for the effectiveness of case-finding tools; however, all clinicians examining children and adults should be alert to physical and behavioral signs and symptoms associated with abuse or neglect. Patients in whom abuse is suspected should receive proper documentation of the incident and physical findings (e.g., photographs, body maps); treatment for physical injuries; arrangements for skilled counseling by a mental health professional; and the telephone numbers of local crisis centers, shelters, and protective service agencies.

■ Victims of family violence are primarily children, female spouses/intimate partners, and older adults. Numerous risk factors for family violence have been identified, although some may be confounded by socioeconomic factors. Factors associated with child abuse or neglect include low income status, low maternal education, non-white race, large family size, young maternal age, single-parent household, parental psychiatric disturbances, and presence of a stepfather. Factors associated with intimate partner violence include young age, low income status, pregnancy, mental health problems, alcohol or substance use by victims or perpetrators, separated or divorced status, and history of childhood sexual and/or physical abuse. Factors associated with the abuse of older adults include increasing age, non-white race, low income status, functional impairment, cognitive disability, substance use, poor emotional state, low self-esteem, cohabitation, and lack of social support.

■ Several instruments to screen parents for child abuse have been studied, but their ability to predict child abuse or neglect is limited. Instruments to screen for intimate partner violence have also been developed, and although some have demonstrated good internal consistency (e.g., the HITS [Hurt, Insulted, Threatened, Screamed at] instrument, the Partner Abuse Interview, and the Women's Experience with Battering [WEB] Scale), none have been validated against measurable outcomes. Only a few screening instruments (the Caregiver Abuse

Screen [CASE] and the Hwalek-Sengstock Elder Abuse Screening Test [HSEAST]) have been developed to identify potential older victims of abuse or their abusive caretakers. Both of these tools correlated well with previously validated instruments when administered in the community, but have not been tested in the primary care clinical setting.[1]

■ Home visit programs directed at high-risk mothers (identified on the basis of sociodemographic risk factors) have improved developmental outcomes and decreased the incidence of child abuse and neglect, as well as decreased rates of maternal criminal activity and drug use.

Reference

1. Nelson HD, Nygren P, Qazi Y. *Screening for Family and Intimate Partner Violence.* Systematic Evidence Review No. 28. (Prepared by the Oregon Health & Science Evidence-based Practice Center under Contract No. 290-97-0018). Rockville, MD: Agency for Healthcare Research and Quality. February 2004. (Available on the AHRQ Web site at: www.ahrq.gov/clinic/serfiles.htm).

This USPSTF recommendation was first published in: *Ann Intern Med.* 2004;140(5):382-386.

Mental Health Conditions and Substance Abuse

Screening and Behavioral Counseling Interventions in Primary Care to Reduce Alcohol Misuse

Summary of Recommendations

The U.S. Preventive Services Task Force (USPSTF) recommends screening and behavioral counseling interventions to reduce alcohol misuse (go to Clinical Considerations) by adults, including pregnant women, in primary care settings. *Rating: B Recommendation.*

The USPSTF concludes that the evidence is insufficient to recommend for or against screening and behavioral counseling interventions to prevent or reduce alcohol misuse by adolescents in primary care settings. *Rating: I Recommendation.*

Clinical Considerations

■ Alcohol misuse includes "risky/hazardous" and "harmful" drinking that places individuals at risk for future problems. "Risky" or "hazardous" drinking has been defined in the United States as more than 7 drinks per week or more than 3 drinks per occasion for women, and more than 14 drinks per week or more than 4 drinks per occasion for men. "Harmful drinking" describes persons who are currently experiencing physical, social, or psychological harm from alcohol use but do not meet criteria for dependence.[1,2] Alcohol abuse and dependence are associated with repeated negative physical, psychological, and social effects from alcohol.[3] The USPSTF did not evaluate the effectiveness of interventions for alcohol dependence because the benefits of these interventions are well established and referral or specialty treatment is recommended for those meeting the diagnostic criteria for dependence.

■ Light to moderate alcohol consumption in middle-aged or older adults has been associated with some health benefits, such as reduced risk for coronary heart disease.[4] Moderate drinking has been defined as 2 standard drinks (e.g., 12 ounces of beer) or less per day for men and 1 drink or less per day for women and persons older than 65,[5] but recent data suggest comparable benefits from as little as 1 drink 3 to 4 times a week.[6]

■ The Alcohol Use Disorders Identification Test (AUDIT) is the most studied screening tool for detecting alcohol-related problems in primary care settings. It is sensitive for detecting alcohol misuse and abuse or dependence and can be used alone or embedded in broader health risk or lifestyle assessments.[7,8] The 4-item CAGE (feeling the need to Cut down, Annoyed by criticism, Guilty about drinking, and need for an Eye-opener in the morning) is the most popular screening test for detecting alcohol abuse or dependence in primary care.[9] The TWEAK, a 5-item scale, and the T-ACE are designed to screen pregnant women for alcohol misuse. They detect lower levels of alcohol consumption that may pose risks during pregnancy.[10] Clinicians can choose screening strategies that are appropriate for their clinical population and setting.[8,11-14] Screening tools are available at the National Institute on Alcohol Abuse and Alcoholism Web site: http://www.niaaa.nih.gov/.

■ Effective interventions to reduce alcohol misuse include an initial counseling session of about 15 minutes, feedback, advice, and goal-setting. Most also include further assistance and follow-up. Multi-contact interventions for patients ranging widely in age (12-75 years) are shown to reduce mean alcohol consumption by 3 to 9 drinks per week, with effects lasting up to 6 to 12 months after the intervention. They can be delivered wholly or in part in the primary care setting, and by one or more members of the health care team, including physician and non-physician practitioners. Resources that help clinicians deliver effective interventions include brief provider training or access to specially trained primary care practitioners or health educators, and the presence of office-level systems supports (prompts, reminders, counseling algorithms, and patient education materials).

■ Primary care screening and behavioral counseling interventions for alcohol misuse can be described with reference to the 5-As behavioral counseling framework: assess alcohol consumption with a brief screening tool followed by clinical assessment as needed; advise patients to reduce alcohol consumption to moderate levels; agree on individual goals for reducing alcohol use or abstinence (if indicated); assist patients with acquiring the motivations, self-help skills, or supports needed for behavior change; and arrange follow-up support and repeated counseling, including referring dependent drinkers for specialty treatment.[15] Common practices that complement this framework include motivational interviewing,[16] the 5 Rs used to treat tobacco use,[17] and assessing readiness to change.[18]

- The optimal interval for screening and intervention is unknown. Patients with past alcohol problems, young adults, and other high-risk groups (e.g., smokers) may benefit most from frequent screening.

- All pregnant women and women contemplating pregnancy should be informed of the harmful effects of alcohol on the fetus. Safe levels of alcohol consumption during pregnancy are not known; therefore, pregnant women are advised to abstain from drinking alcohol. More research into the efficacy of primary care screening and behavioral intervention for alcohol misuse among pregnant women is needed.

- The benefits of behavioral intervention for preventing or reducing alcohol misuse in adolescents are not known. The CRAFFT questionnaire was recently validated for screening adolescents for substance abuse in the primary care setting.[19] The benefits of screening this population will need to be evaluated as more effective interventions become available in the primary care setting.

References

1. Reid MC, Fiellin DA, O'Connor PG. Hazardous and harmful alcohol consumption in primary care. *Arch Intern Med.* 1999;159(15):1681-1689.

2. *WHO. The ICD-10 Classification of Mental and Behavioural Disorders: Clinical Descriptions and Diagnostic Guidelines.* Geneva, Switzerland: World Health Organization; 1992.

3. American Psychiatric Association. *Diagnostic and Statistical Manual of Mental Disorders.* 4th Ed. Washington, DC: American Psychiatric Association; 1994.

4. Tenth special report to the U.S. Congress on alcohol and health from the Secretary of Health and Human Services. U.S. Department of Health and Human Services. Washington, DC: National Institutes of Health, National Institute on Alcohol Abuse and Alcoholism (NIAAA). NIH Publication No. 00-1583; June 2000.

5. The Physician's Guide to Helping Patients with Alcohol Problems. National Institute on Alcohol Abuse and Alcoholism (NIAAA). NIH Pub. No. 95-3769. Bethesda, MD; 1995.

6. Mukamal KJ, Conigrave KM, Mittleman MA, et al. Roles of drinking pattern and type of alcohol consumed in coronary heart disease in men. *N Engl J Med.* 2003;348(2):109-118.

7. Saunders JB, Aasland OG, Babor TF, de la Fuente JR, Grant M. Development of the Alcohol Use Disorders Identification Test (AUDIT): WHO Collaborative Project on Early Detection of Persons with Harmful Alcohol Consumption-II. *Addiction.* 1993;88(6):791-804.

8. Fiellin DA, Reid MC, O'Connor PG. Screening for alcohol problems in primary care: a systematic review. *Arch Intern Med.* 2000;160(13):1977-1989.

9. Ewing JA. Detecting Alcoholism: The CAGE questionnaire. *JAMA.* 1984;252(14):1905-1907.

10. Chang G. Alcohol-screening instruments for pregnant women. *Alcohol Res Health.* 2001;25(3):204-209.

11. Babor TF, Higgins-Biddle JC. *Brief Intervention for Hazardous and Harmful Drinking.* A Manual for Use in Primary Care. World Health Organization; 2001.

12. Training Physicians in Techniques for Alcohol Screening and Brief Intervention. National Institutes of Health. National Institute on Alcohol Abuse and Alcoholism (NIAAA). Bethesda, MD; 1997.

13. Whaley SE, O'Conner MJ. Increasing the report of alcohol use among low-income pregnant women. *American Journal of Health Promot.* 2003;17(6):369-372.

14. Fleming MF. *Identification of at-Risk Drinking and Intervention with Women of Childbearing Age: Guide for Primary Care Providers.* National Institute on Alcohol Abuse and Alcoholism (NIAAA). NIH. Bethesda, Maryland; 2000.

15. Whitlock EP, Orleans CT, Pender N, Allan J. Evaluating primary care behavioral counseling interventions. An evidence-based approach. *Am J Prev Med.* 2002;22(4):267-284.

16. Miller WR, Rollnick S, Con K. *Motivational Interviewing: Preparing People for Change.* 2nd ed. New York: Guilford Press; 2002.

17. Anderson JE, Jorenby DE, Scott WJ, Fiore MC. Treating tobacco use and dependence: an evidence-based clinical practice guideline for tobacco cessation. *Chest.* 2002;121(3):932-941.

18. Prochaska JO, Velicer WF. The transtheoretical model of health behavior change. *Am J Health Promot.* 1997;12(1):38-48.

19. Knight JR, Sherritt L, Harris SK, Gates EC, Chang G. Validity of brief alcohol screening tests among adolescents: A comparison of the AUDIT, POSIT, CAGE, and CRAFFT. *Alcohol Clin Exp Res.* 2003;27(1):67-73.

This USPSTF recommendation was first published in: *Ann Intern Med.* 2004;140:555-557.

Screening for Dementia

Summary of Recommendation

The U.S. Preventive Services Task Force (USPSTF) concludes that the evidence is insufficient to recommend for or against routine screening for dementia in older adults. *Rating: I Recommendation.*

Clinical Considerations

■ The Mini-Mental Status Examination (MMSE) is the best-studied instrument for screening for cognitive impairment. When the MMSE is used to screen unselected patients, the predictive value of a positive result is only fair. The accuracy of the MMSE depends upon a person's age and educational level: using an arbitrary cut-point may potentially lead to more false-positives among older people with lower educational levels, and more false-negatives among younger people with higher educational levels. Tests that assess functional limitations rather than cognitive impairment, such as the Functional Activities Questionnaire (FAQ), can detect dementia with sensitivity and specificity comparable to that of the MMSE.

■ Early recognition of cognitive impairment, in addition to helping make diagnostic and treatment decisions, allows clinicians to anticipate problems the patients may have in understanding and adhering to recommended therapy. This information may also be useful to the patient's caregiver(s) and family member(s) in helping to anticipate and plan for future problems that may develop as a result of progression of cognitive impairment.

■ Although current evidence does not support routine screening of patients in whom cognitive impairment is not otherwise suspected, clinicians should assess cognitive function whenever cognitive impairment or deterioration is suspected, based on direct observation, patient report, or concerns raised by family members, friends, or caretakers.

This USPSTF recommendation was first published in: *Ann Intern Med.* 2003;138:925-926.

Screening for Depression

Summary of Recommendations

The U.S. Preventive Services Task Force (USPSTF) recommends screening adults for depression in clinical practices that have systems in place to assure accurate diagnosis, effective treatment, and follow-up. *Rating: B Recommendation.*

The USPSTF concludes the evidence is insufficient to recommend for or against routine screening of children or adolescents for depression. *Rating: I Recommendation.*

Clinical Considerations

■ Many formal screening tools are available (e.g., the Zung Self-Assessment Depression Scale, Beck Depression Inventory, General Health Questionnaire [GHQ], Center for Epidemiologic Study Depression Scale [CES-D]).[1] Asking 2 simple questions about mood and anhedonia ("Over the past 2 weeks, have you felt down, depressed, or hopeless?" and "Over the past 2 weeks, have you felt little interest or pleasure in doing things?") may be as effective as using longer instruments.[2] There is little evidence to recommend one screening method over another, so clinicians can choose the method that best fits their personal preference, the patient population served, and the practice setting.

■ All positive screening tests should trigger full diagnostic interviews that use standard diagnostic criteria (ie, those from the fourth edition of the Diagnostic and Statistical Manual of Mental Disorders [DSM-IV]) to determine the presence or absence of specific depressive disorders, such as major depression and/or dysthymia.[3] The severity of depression and comorbid psychological problems (e.g., anxiety, panic attacks, or substance abuse) should be addressed.

■ Many risk factors for depression (e.g., female sex, family history of depression, unemployment, and chronic disease) are common, but the presence of risk factors alone cannot distinguish depressed from nondepressed patients.

■ The optimal interval for screening is unknown. Recurrent screening may be most productive in patients with a history of depression, unexplained somatic symptoms, comorbid psychological conditions (e.g., panic disorder or generalized anxiety), substance abuse, or chronic pain.

■ Clinical practices that screen for depression should have systems in place to ensure that positive screening results are followed by accurate diagnosis, effective treatment, and careful follow-up. Benefits from screening are unlikely to be realized unless such systems are functioning well.

■ Treatment may include antidepressants or specific psychotherapeutic approaches (e.g., cognitive behavioral therapy or brief psychosocial counseling), alone or in combination.

■ The benefits of routinely screening children and adolescents for depression are not known. The existing literature suggests that screening tests perform reasonably well in adolescents and that treatments are effective, but the clinical impact of routine depression screening has not been studied in pediatric populations in primary care settings. Clinicians should remain alert for possible signs of depression in younger patients. The predictive value of positive screening tests is lower in children and adolescents than in adults, and research on the effectiveness of primary care-based interventions for depression in this age group is limited.

References

1. Williams JW, Hitchcock Noel P, Cordes JA, Ramirez G, Pignone M. Rational clinical examination. Is this patient clinically depressed? *JAMA.* 2002;287:1160-1167.

2. Whooley MA, Avins AL, Miranda J, Browner WS. Case-finding instruments for depression: Two questions are as good as many. *J Gen Intern Med.* 1997;12:439-445.

3. American Psychiatric Association. Diagnostic and Statistical Manual of Mental Disorders: DSM-IV. 4th ed. Washington, DC: American Psychiatric Association; 1994.

This USPSTF recommendation was first published in: *Ann Intern Med.* 2002;136:760-764.

Screening for Suicide Risk

Summary of Recommendation

The U.S. Preventive Services Task Force (USPSTF) concludes that the evidence is insufficient to recommend for or against routine screening by primary care clinicians to detect suicide risk in the general population. *Rating: I Recommendation.*

Clinical Considerations

■ The strongest risk factors for attempted suicide include mood disorders or other mental disorders, comorbid substance abuse disorders, history of deliberate self-harm (DSH), and a history of suicide attempts. DSH refers to intentionally initiated acts of self-harm with a non-fatal outcome (including self-poisoning and self-injury). Suicide risk is assessed along a continuum ranging from suicidal ideation alone (relatively less severe) to suicidal ideation with a plan (more severe). Suicidal ideation with a specific plan of action is associated with a significant risk for attempted suicide.

■ Screening instruments are commonly used in specialty clinics and mental health settings. The test characteristics of most commonly-used screening instruments (Scale for Suicide Ideation [SSI], Scale for Suicide Ideation-Worst [SSI-W], and the Suicidal Ideation Questionnaire [SIQ]) have not been validated to assess suicide risk in primary care settings. There has been limited testing of the

Symptom-Driven Diagnostic System for Primary Care (SDDS-PC) screening instrument in a primary care setting.

This USPSTF recommendation was first published in: *Ann Intern Med.* 2004;140:820-821.

Counseling to Prevent Tobacco Use and Tobacco-Caused Disease

Summary of Recommendations

The U.S. Preventive Services Task Force (USPSTF) strongly recommends that clinicians screen all adults for tobacco use and provide tobacco cessation interventions for those who use tobacco products. *Rating: A Recommendation.*

The USPSTF strongly recommends that clinicians screen all pregnant women for tobacco use and provide augmented pregnancy-tailored counseling to those who smoke. *Rating: A Recommendation.*

The USPSTF concludes that the evidence is insufficient to recommend for or against routine screening for tobacco use or interventions to prevent and treat tobacco use and dependence among children or adolescents. *Rating: I Recommendation.*

Clinical Considerations

■ Brief tobacco cessation counseling interventions, including screening, brief counseling (3 minutes or less), and/or pharmacotherapy, have proven to increase tobacco abstinence rates, although there is a dose-response relationship between quit rates and the intensity of counseling. Effective interventions may be delivered by a variety of primary care clinicians.

120

- The 5-A behavioral counseling framework provides a useful strategy for engaging patients in smoking cessation discussions:

    1. **Ask** about tobacco use.

    2. **Advise** to quit through clear personalized messages.

    3. **Assess** willingness to quit.

    4. **Assist** to quit.

    5. **Arrange** follow-up and support.

  Helpful aspects of counseling include providing problem-solving guidance for smokers to develop a plan to quit and to overcome common barriers to quitting and providing social support within and outside of treatment. Common practices that complement this framework include motivational interviewing, the 5-R's used to treat tobacco use (*relevance, risks, rewards, roadblocks, repetition*), assessing readiness to change, and more intensive counseling and/or referrals for quitters needing extra help.[1-3] Telephone "quit lines" have also been found to be an effective adjunct to counseling or medical therapy.[4]

- Clinics that implement screening systems designed to regularly identify and document a patient's tobacco use status increased their rates of clinician intervention, although there is limited evidence for the impact of screening systems on tobacco cessation rates.[5]

121

■ FDA-approved pharmacotherapy that has been identified as safe and effective for treating tobacco dependence includes several forms of nicotine replacement therapy (ie, nicotine gum, nicotine transdermal patches, nicotine inhaler, and nicotine nasal spray) and sustained-release bupropion. Other medications, including clonidine and nortriptyline, have been found to be efficacious and may be considered.

■ Augmented pregnancy-tailored counseling (e.g., 5-15 minutes) and self-help materials are recommended for pregnant smokers, as brief interventions are less effective in this population. There is limited evidence to evaluate the safety or efficacy of pharmacotherapy during pregnancy. Tobacco cessation at any point during pregnancy can yield important health benefits for the mother and the baby, but there are limited data about the optimal timing or frequency of counseling interventions during pregnancy.

■ There is little evidence addressing the effectiveness of screening and counseling children or adolescents to prevent the initiation of tobacco use and to promote its cessation in a primary care setting, but clinicians may use their discretion in conducting tobacco-related discussions with this population, since the majority of adult smokers begin tobacco use as children or adolescents.

References

1. Miller W, Rolnick S. *Motivational Interviewing: Preparing People to Change Addictive Behavior.* New York: Guilford, 1991.

2. Anderson JE, Jorenby DE, Scott WJ, Fiore MC. Treating tobacco use and dependence: an evidence-based clinical practice guideline for tobacco cessation. *Chest.* 2002;121(3):932-941.

3. Prochaska JO, Velicer WF. The transtheoretical model of health behavior change. *Am J Health Promot.* 1997;12(1):38-48.

4. CDC. Strategies for reducing exposure to environmental tobacco smoke, tobacco-use cessation, and reducing initiation in communities and health-care systems. A report on recommendations of the Task Force on Community Preventive Services. *MMWR.* 2000:49(No. RR-12);1-11.

5. Fiore MC, Bailey WC, Cohen SJ, et al. *Treating Tobacco Use and Dependence.* Rockville MD: Department of Health and Human Services, Public Health Service, 2000.

This USPSTF recommendation was first published by: Agency for Healthcare Research and Quality, Rockville, MD. November 2003. http://www.ahrq.gov/clinic/uspstf/uspstbac.htm.

Metabolic, Nutritional, and Endocrine Conditions

Behavioral Counseling in Primary Care to Promote a Healthy Diet

Summary of Recommendations

The U.S. Preventive Services Task Force (USPSTF) concludes that the evidence is insufficient to recommend for or against routine behavioral counseling to promote a healthy diet in unselected patients in primary care settings. *Rating: I Recommendation.*

The USPSTF recommends intensive behavioral dietary counseling for adult patients with hyperlipidemia and other known risk factors for cardiovascular and diet-related chronic disease. Intensive counseling can be delivered by primary care clinicians or by referral to other specialists, such as nutritionists or dietitians. *Rating: B Recommendation.*

Clinical Considerations

- Several brief dietary assessment questionnaires have been validated for use in the primary care setting.[1,2] These instruments can identify dietary counseling needs, guide interventions, and monitor changes in patients' dietary patterns. However, these instruments are susceptible to the bias of the respondent. Therefore, when used to evaluate the efficacy of counseling, efforts to verify self-reported information are recommended since patients receiving dietary interventions may be more likely to report positive changes in dietary behavior than control patients.[3-6]

■ Effective interventions combine nutrition education with behaviorally-oriented counseling to help patients acquire the skills, motivation, and support needed to alter their daily eating patterns and food preparation practices. Examples of behaviorally-oriented counseling interventions include teaching self monitoring, training to overcome common barriers to selecting a healthy diet, helping patients to set their own goals, providing guidance in shopping and food preparation, role playing, and arranging for intra-treatment social support. In general, these interventions can be described with reference to the 5-A behavioral counseling framework[7]:

1. **Assess** dietary practices and related risk factors.

2. **Advise** to change dietary practices.

3. **Agree** on individual diet change goals.

4. **Assist** to change dietary practices or address motivational barriers.

5. **Arrange** regular follow-up and support or refer to more intensive behavioral nutritional counseling (e.g., medical nutrition therapy) if needed.

126

- Two approaches appear promising for the general
  population of adult patients in primary care
  settings:

  1. Medium-intensity face-to-face dietary
     counseling (2 to 3 group or individual
     sessions) delivered by a dietitian or
     nutritionist or by a specially trained primary
     care physician or nurse practitioner.

  2. Lower-intensity interventions that involve 5
     minutes or less of primary care provider
     counseling supplemented by patient self-
     help materials, telephone counseling, or
     other interactive health communications.

  However, more research is needed to assess the
  long-term efficacy of these treatments and the
  balance of benefits and harms.

- The largest effect of dietary counseling in
  asymptomatic adults has been observed with more
  intensive interventions (multiple sessions lasting 30
  minutes or longer) among patients with
  hyperlipidemia or hypertension, and among others
  at increased risk for diet-related chronic disease.
  Effective interventions include individual or group
  counseling delivered by nutritionists, dietitians, or
  specially trained primary care practitioners or health
  educators in the primary care setting or in other
  clinical settings by referral. Most studies of these
  interventions have enrolled selected patients, many
  of whom had known diet-related risk factors such as
  hyperlipidemia or hypertension. Similar approaches

may be effective with unselected adult patients, but adherence to dietary advice may be lower, and health benefits smaller, than in patients who have been told they are at higher risk for diet-related chronic disease.[8]

■ Office-level systems supports (prompts, reminders, and counseling algorithms) have been found to significantly improve the delivery of appropriate dietary counseling by primary care clinicians.[9-11]

■ Possible harms of dietary counseling have not been well defined or measured. Some have raised concerns that if patients focus only on reducing total fat intake without attention to reducing caloric intake, an increase in carbohydrate intake (e.g., reduced-fat or low-fat food products) may lead to weight gain, elevated triglyceride levels, or insulin resistance. Nationally, obesity rates have increased despite declining fat consumption, but studies did not consistently examine effects of counseling on outcomes such as caloric intake and weight.

■ Little is known about effective dietary counseling for children or adolescents in the primary care setting. Most studies of nutritional interventions for children and adolescents have focused on non-clinical settings (such as schools) or have used physiologic outcomes such as cholesterol or weight rather than more comprehensive measures of a healthy diet.[12,13]

References

1. Calfas KJ, Zabinski MF, Rupp J. Practical nutrition assessment in primary care settings: a review. *Am J Prev Med.* 2000;18(4):289-299.

2. Rockett HR, Colditz GA. Assessing diets of children and adolescents. *Am J Clin Nutr.* 1997;65(4):1116-1122.

3. Beresford SA, Farmer EM, Feingold L, Graves KL, Sumner SK, Baker RM. Evaluation of a self-help dietary intervention in a primary care setting. *Am J Public Health.* 1992;82(1):79-84.

4. Coates RJ, Bowen DJ, Kristal AR, et al. The Women's Health Trial Feasibility Study in Minority Populations: changes in dietary intakes. *Am J Epidemiol.* 1999;149(12):1104-1112.

5. Kristal AR, Curry SJ, Shattuck AL, Feng Z, Li S. A randomized trial of a tailored, self-help dietary intervention: the Puget Sound Eating Patterns study. *Prev Med.* 2000;31(4):380-389.

6. Little P, Barnett J, Margetts B, et al. The validity of dietary assessment in general practice. *J Epidemiol Commun Health.* 1999;53(3):165-172.

7. Whitlock EP, Orleans CT, Pender N, Allan J. Evaluating primary care behavioral counseling interventions: an evidence-based approach. *Am J Prev Med.* 2002;22(4):267-284.

8. Maskarinec G, Chan CL, Meng L, Franke AA, Cooney RV. Exploring the feasibility and effects of a high-fruit and -vegetable diet in healthy women. *Cancer Epidemiol Biomarkers Prev.* 1999;8(10):919-924.

9. Beresford SA, Curry SJ, Kristal AR, Lazovich D, Feng Z, Wagner EH. A dietary intervention in primary care

practice: the Eating Patterns Study. *Am J Public Health.* 1997;87(4):610-616.

10. Ockene IS, Hebert JR, Ockene JK, et al. Effect of physician-delivered nutrition counseling training and an office-support program on saturated fat intake, weight, and serum lipid measurements in a hyperlipidemic population: Worcester Area Trial for Counseling in Hyperlipidemia (WATCH). *Arch Int Med.* 1999;159(7):725-731.

11. Ockene IS, Hebert JR, Ockene JK, Merriam PA, Hurley TG, Saperia GM. Effect of training and a structured office practice on physician-delivered nutrition counseling: the Worcester-Area Trial for Counseling in Hyperlipidemia (WATCH). *Am J Prev Med.* 1996;12(4):252-258.

12. Obarzanek E, Hunsberger SA, Van Horn L, et al. Safety of a fat-reduced diet: the Dietary Intervention Study in Children (DISC). *Pediatrics.* 1997;100(1):51-59.

13. Obarzanek E, Kimm SY, Barton BA, et al. Long-term safety and efficacy of a cholesterol-lowering diet in children with elevated low-density lipoprotein cholesterol: seven-year results of the Dietary Intervention Study in Children (DISC). *Pediatrics.* 2001;107(2):256-264.

This USPSTF recommendation was first published in: *Am J Prev Med.* 2003;24(1):93-100.

Screening for Hemochromatosis

Summary of Recommendation

The U.S. Preventive Services Task Force (USPSTF) recommends against routine genetic screening for hereditary hemochromatosis in the asymptomatic general population. *Rating: D Recommendation.*

Clinical Considerations

■ This recommendation applies to asymptomatic persons. This recommendation does not include individuals with signs or symptoms that would include hereditary hemochromatosis in the differential diagnosis. Furthermore, it does not include individuals with a family history of clinically detected or screening-detected probands for hereditary hemochromatosis.

■ Clinically important disease due to hereditary hemochromatosis appears to be rare. Even among individuals with mutations on the hemochromatosis *(HFE)* gene, it appears that only a small subset will develop symptoms of hemochromatosis. An even smaller proportion of these individuals will develop advanced stages of clinical disease.

■ Clinically recognized hereditary hemochromatosis is primarily associated with the *HFE* mutation C282Y. Although this is a relatively common mutation in the U.S. population, great racial and ethnic variations exist. The frequency of homozygosity is 4.4 per 1000 among white persons, with much lower frequencies among Hispanic persons (0.27 per 1000), black persons (0.14 per 1000), and Asian-American persons (<0.001 per 1000). Screening of family members of probands identifies the highest prevalence of undetected C282Y homozygotes (23 percent of all family members tested), particularly among siblings (33 percent homozygosity).

■ The natural history of disease due to hereditary hemochromatosis is not well understood but appears to vary considerably among individuals. Clinically recognized hereditary hemochromatosis is about twice as common in men as in women. Iron accumulation and disease expression are modified by environmental factors, including blood loss or donation, alcohol use, diet, and infections such as viral hepatitis.

■ Among C282Y homozygotes newly identified in the general population by genotypic screening, 6 percent of those undergoing further evaluation had cirrhosis (representing 1.4 percent of all newly screening-identified C282Y homozygotes). Cirrhosis is a serious, late-stage disease development, and its prevention would be a major goal of screening and treatment.

■ Individuals with a family member, especially a sibling, who is known to have hereditary hemochromatosis may be more likely to develop symptoms. These individuals should be counseled regarding genotyping, with further diagnostic testing as warranted as part of case-finding.

■ In addition to genotyping, more common laboratory testing can sometimes identify iron overload. Clinical screening with these laboratory tests, or phenotypic screening, was not included in the evidence synthesis on which this recommendation is based. Genotyping primarily focuses on the identification of the C282Y mutation on *HFE*. While other mutations exist, C282Y homozygosity is most commonly associated with clinical manifestations. Identifying an individual with the genotypic predisposition does not accurately predict the future risk for disease manifestation.

■ Therapeutic phlebotomy is the primary treatment for hemochromatosis. Treated individuals report inconsistent improvement of their signs and symptoms. It is uncertain whether cirrhosis at diagnosis confers a worse prognosis based on the potential lack of reversibility of liver damage. Recent research reports survival rates in treated individuals with or without cirrhosis that are similar to rates in healthy controls. The degree to which clinically important manifestations can be averted remains uncertain, as does the optimal time for early treatment.

References

1. Niederau C, Fisher R, Purschel A, Stremmel W, Haussinger D, Strohmeyer G. Long-term survival in patients with hereditary hemochromatosis. *Gastroenterology.* 1996;110:1107-1119.

2. Powell LW, Dixon JL, Ramm GA, Purdie DM, Lincoln DJ, Anderson GJ, et al. Screening for hemochromatosis in asymptomatic subjects with or without a family history. *Arch Int Med.* 2006;166:294-301.

3. Adams PC, Speechley M, Kertesz AE. Long-term survival analysis in hereditary hemochromatosis. *Gastroenterology.* 1991;101:368-372.

4. Bomford A, Williams R. Long term results of venesection therapy in idiopathic haemochromatosis. *Q J Med.* 1976;45:611-623.

This USPSTF recommendation was first published in *Ann Intern Med.* 2006;145:204-208.

Hormone Therapy for the Prevention of Chronic Conditions in Postmenopausal Women

Summary of Recommendations

The U.S. Preventive Services Task Force (USPSTF) recommends against the routine use of combined estrogen and progestin for the prevention of chronic conditions in postmenopausal women. *Rating: D recommendation.*

The USPSTF recommends against the routine use of unopposed estrogen for the prevention of chronic conditions in postmenopausal women who have had a hysterectomy. *Rating: D recommendation.*

Clinical Considerations

■ The balance of benefits and harms for a woman will be influenced by her personal preferences, her risks for specific chronic diseases, and the presence of menopausal symptoms. A shared decisionmaking approach to preventing chronic diseases in perimenopausal and postmenopausal women involves consideration of individual risk factors and preferences in selecting effective interventions for reducing the risks for fracture, heart disease, and cancer. See other USPSTF recommendations for prevention of chronic diseases (screening for osteoporosis, high blood pressure, lipid disorders, breast cancer, and colorectal cancer; and counseling

135

to prevent tobacco use) available at:
www.preventiveservices.ahrq.gov.

■ The USPSTF did not consider the use of hormone
therapy for the management of menopausal
symptoms, which is the subject of
recommendations by other expert groups. Women
and their clinicians should discuss the balance of
risks and benefits before deciding to initiate or
continue hormone therapy for menopausal
symptoms. For example, for combined estrogen and
progestin, some risks (such as the risks for venous
thromboembolism, coronary heart disease [CHD],
and stroke) arise within the first 1 to 2 years of
therapy, and other risks (such as the risk for breast
cancer) appear to increase with longer-term
hormone therapy. The populations of women using
hormone therapy for symptom relief may differ
from those who would use hormone therapy for
prevention of chronic disease (e.g., age differences).
Other expert groups have recommended that
women who decide to take hormone therapy to
relieve menopausal symptoms use the lowest
effective dose for the shortest possible time.

■ Although estrogen alone or in combination with
progestin reduces the risk for fractures in women,
other effective medications (e.g., bisphosphonates
and calcitonin) are available for treating women
with low bone density to prevent fractures. The

role of chemopreventive agents in preventing fractures in women without low bone density is unclear. The USPSTF addressed screening for osteoporosis in postmenopausal women in 2002.[1]

■ Unopposed estrogen increases the risk for endometrial cancer in women who have an intact uterus. Clinicians should use a shared decision-making approach when discussing the possibility of using unopposed estrogen in women who have not had a hysterectomy.[2]

References

1. U.S. Preventive Services Task Force. Screening for osteoporosis in postmenopausal women: recommendations from the U.S. Preventive Services Task Force. *Ann Intern Med.* 137(6):526-528.

2. Sheridan SL, Harris RP, Woolf SH, for the Shared Decisionmaking Workgroup, Third U.S. Preventive Services Task Force. Shared decision-making about screening and chemoprevention: a suggested approach from the U. S. Preventive Services Task Force. *Am J Prev Med.* 2004;26(1):56-66.

This USPSTF recommendation was first published in: *Ann Intern Med.* 2005;142:855-860.

Screening for Iron Deficiency Anemia—Including Iron Supplementation for Children and Pregnant Women

Summary of Recommendations

The U.S. Preventive Services Task Force (USPSTF) concludes that evidence is insufficient to recommend for or against routine screening for iron deficiency anemia in asymptomatic children aged 6 to 12 months. *Rating: I Recommendation.*

The USPSTF recommends routine screening for iron deficiency anemia in asymptomatic pregnant women. *Rating: B Recommendation.*

The USPSTF recommends routine iron supplementation for asymptomatic children aged 6 to 12 months who are at increased risk for iron deficiency anemia (see Clinical Considerations for a discussion of increased risk). *Rating: B Recommendation.*

The USPSTF concludes that evidence is insufficient to recommend for or against routine iron supplementation for asymptomatic children aged 6 to 12 months who are at average risk for iron deficiency anemia. *Rating: I Recommendation.*

The USPSTF concludes that evidence is insufficient to recommend for or against routine iron supplementation for non-anemic pregnant women. *Rating: I Recommendation.*

Clinical Considerations

■ These USPSTF recommendations address screening for iron deficiency anemia and iron supplementation in children aged 6 to 12 months who are at increased risk and average risk, in asymptomatic pregnant women, and in non-anemic pregnant women. Infants younger than 6 months of age, older children, non-pregnant women, and men are not addressed.

■ Iron deficiency anemia can be defined as iron deficiency (abnormal values for serum ferritin, transferrin saturation, and free erythrocyte protoporphyrin) with a low hemoglobin or hematocrit value. Iron deficiency is much more common than iron deficiency anemia and is part of a continuum that ranges from iron depletion to iron deficiency anemia. Many of the negative health outcomes of iron deficiency are associated with its extreme manifestation, iron deficiency anemia. Iron deficiency has also been associated with negative neurodevelopmental outcomes in children.

■ Other causes of anemia vary by population and include other nutritional deficiencies, abnormal hemoglobin (e.g., thalassemia), enzyme defects, and anemia associated with acute and chronic infections.

■ In the U.S., race, income, education, and other socioeconomic factors are associated with iron deficiency and iron deficiency anemia. Individuals considered to be at high risk for iron deficiency include adult females, recent immigrants, and among adolescent females, fad dieters, and those who are obese. Premature and low birth weight infants are also at increased risk for iron deficiency.

■ Venous hemoglobin is more accurate than capillary hemoglobin for identifying anemia. Ferritin has the highest sensitivity and specificity for diagnosing iron deficiency in anemic patients.

■ Iron deficiency anemia is usually treated with oral iron preparations. The likelihood that iron deficiency anemia identified by screening will respond to treatment is unclear because many families do not adhere to treatment and because the rate of spontaneous resolution is high. 97 percent of infant formula sold in the U.S. is iron-fortified. Substantial reductions in the incidence of iron deficiency and iron deficiency anemia have been demonstrated in healthy infants fed iron-fortified formula or iron-fortified cereal, compared with infants fed cow's milk or unfortified formula.

■ Iron supplements accounted for 30 percent of fatal pediatric pharmaceutical overdoses occurring between 1983 and 1990, and iron poisoning has been observed even in the context of controlled trials in which parents were instructed in the safe storage and use of iron products. A reduction in deaths of children due to iron overdose was observed when unit-dose packaging was required between 1998 and 2002; this requirement was overturned by the courts in 2003.

References

1. Helfand M, Freeman M, Nygren P, Walker M. *Screening for Iron Deficiency Anemia in Childhood and Pregnancy: Update of 1996 USPSTF Review.* Evidence Synthesis No. 43 (prepared by the Oregon Evidence-based Practice Center under Contract No. 290-02-0024). Rockville, MD: Agency for Healthcare Research and Quality. April 2006. (Available on the AHRQ Web site at: http://www.ahrq.gov/clinic/uspstfix.htm.)

2. Martins S, Logan S, Gilbert R. Iron therapy for improving psychomotor development and cognitive function in children under the age of three with iron deficiency. *The Cochrane Database of Systematic Reviews.* 2001, Issue 2. Art. No.: CD001444. DOI: 10.1002/14651858.CD001444. (Available at http://www.mrw.interscience.wiley.com/cochrane/clsysrev/articles/CD001444/frame.html.)

This USPSTF recommendation was first published by: Agency for Healthcare Research and Quality, Rockville, MD. May 2006. http://www.ahrq.gov/clinic/uspstf06/ironsc/ironrs.htm.

Screening for Obesity in Adults

Summary of Recommendations

The U.S. Preventive Services Task Force (USPSTF) recommends that clinicians screen all adult patients for obesity and offer intensive counseling and behavioral interventions to promote sustained weight loss for obese adults. *Rating: B Recommendation.*

The USPSTF concludes that the evidence is insufficient to recommend for or against the use of moderate- or low-intensity counseling together with behavioral interventions to promote sustained weight loss in obese adults. *Rating: I Recommendation.*

The USPSTF concludes that the evidence is insufficient to recommend for or against the use of counseling of any intensity and behavioral interventions to promote sustained weight loss in overweight adults. *Rating: I Recommendation.*

Clinical Considerations

- A number of techniques, such as bioelectrical impedance, dual-energy x-ray absorptiometry, and total body water can measure body fat, but it is impractical to use them routinely. Body mass index (BMI), which is simply weight adjusted for height, is a more practical and widely-used method to screen for obesity. Increased BMI is associated with an increase in adverse health effects. Central adiposity increases the risk for cardiovascular and other diseases independent of obesity. Clinicians may use the waist circumference as a measure of central adiposity. Men with waist circumferences greater than 102 cm (> 40 inches) and women with waist circumferences greater than 88 cm (> 35 inches) are at increased risk for cardiovascular disease. The waist circumference thresholds are not reliable for patients with a BMI greater than 35.

■ Expert committees have issued guidelines defining overweight and obesity based on BMI. Persons with a BMI between 25 and 29.9 are overweight and those with a BMI of 30 and above are obese. There are 3 classes of obesity: class I (BMI 30-34.9), class II (BMI 35-39.9), and class III (BMI 40 and above). BMI is calculated either as weight in pounds divided by height in inches squared multiplied by 703, or as weight in kilograms divided by height in meters squared. The National Institutes of Health (NIH) provides a BMI calculator at www.nhlbisupport.com/bmi/ and a table at www.nhlbi.nih.gov/guidelines/obesity/bmi_tbl.htm.

■ The most effective interventions combine nutrition education and diet and exercise counseling with behavioral strategies to help patients acquire the skills and supports needed to change eating patterns and to become physically active. The 5-A framework (Assess, Advise, Agree, Assist, and Arrange) has been used in behavioral counseling interventions such as smoking cessation and may be a useful tool to help clinicians guide interventions for weight loss. Initial interventions paired with maintenance interventions help ensure that weight loss will be sustained over time.

■ It is advisable to refer obese patients to programs that offer intensive counseling and behavioral interventions for optimal weight loss. The USPSTF defined intensity of counseling by the frequency of the intervention. A high-intensity intervention is more than 1 person-to-person (individual or group) session per month for at least the first 3 months of the intervention. A medium-intensity intervention is a monthly intervention, and anything less frequent is a low-intensity intervention. There are limited data on the best place for these interventions to occur and on the composition of the multidisciplinary team that should deliver high-intensity interventions.

■ The USPSTF concluded that the evidence on the effectiveness of interventions with obese people may not be generalizable to adults who are overweight but not obese. The evidence for the effectiveness of interventions for weight loss among overweight adults, compared with obese adults, is limited.

■ Orlistat and sibutramine, approved for weight loss by the Food and Drug Administration, can produce modest weight loss (2.6-4.8 kg) that can be sustained for at least 2 years if the medication is continued. The adverse effects of orlistat include fecal urgency, oily spotting, and flatulence; the adverse effects of sibutramine include an increase in blood pressure and heart rate. There are no data on the long-term (longer than 2 years) benefits or adverse effects of these drugs. Experts recommend that pharmacological treatment of obesity be used only as part of a program that also includes lifestyle modification interventions, such as intensive diet and/or exercise counseling and behavioral interventions.

■ There is fair to good evidence to suggest that surgical interventions such as gastric bypass, vertical banded gastroplasty, and adjustable gastric banding can produce substantial weight loss (28 to > 40 kg) in patients with class III obesity. Clinical guidelines developed by the National Heart, Lung, and Blood Institute (NHLBI) Expert Panel on the identification, evaluation, and treatment of overweight and obesity in adults recommend that these procedures be reserved for patients with class III obesity and for patients with class II obesity who have at least 1 other obesity-related illness. The postoperative mortality rate for these procedures is 0.2 percent. Other complications include wound infection, re-operation, vitamin deficiency, diarrhea, and hemorrhage. Re-operation may be necessary in up to 25 percent of patients. Patients should receive a psychological evaluation prior to undergoing these procedures. The long-term health effects of surgery for obesity are not well characterized.

■ The data supporting the effectiveness of interventions to promote weight loss are derived mostly from women, especially white women. The effectiveness of the interventions is less well established in other populations, including the elderly. The USPSTF believes that, although the data are limited, these interventions may be used with obese men, physiologically mature older adolescents, and diverse populations, taking into account cultural and other individual factors.

This USPSTF recommendation was first published in: *Ann Intern Med.* 2003;139:930-932.

Behavioral Counseling in Primary Care to Promote Physical Activity

Summary of Recommendation

The U.S. Preventive Services Task Force (USPSTF) concludes that the evidence is insufficient to recommend for or against behavioral counseling in primary care settings to promote physical activity. *Rating: I Recommendation.*

Clinical Considerations

■ Regular physical activity helps prevent cardiovascular disease, hypertension, type 2 diabetes, obesity, and osteoporosis. It may also decrease all-cause morbidity and lengthen life-span.[1]

■ Benefits of physical activity are seen at even modest levels of activity, such as walking or bicycling 30 minutes per day on most days of the week. Benefits increase with increasing levels of activity.[2]

■ Whether routine counseling and follow-up by primary care physicians results in increased physical activity among their adult patients is unclear. Existing studies limit the conclusions that can be drawn about efficacy, effectiveness, and feasibility of primary care physical activity counseling. Most studies have tested brief, minimal, and low-intensity primary care interventions, such as 3 to 5 minute counseling sessions in the context of a routine clinical visit.

147

■ Multi-component interventions combining provider advice with behavioral interventions to facilitate and reinforce healthy levels of physical activity appear the most promising. Such interventions often include patient goal setting, written exercise prescriptions, individually tailored physical activity regimens, and mailed or telephone follow-up assistance provided by specially trained staff. Linking primary care patients to community-based physical activity and fitness programs may enhance the effectiveness of primary care clinician counseling.[3]

■ Potential harms of physical activity counseling have not been well defined or studied. They may include muscle and fall-related injuries or cardiovascular events.[4] It is unclear whether more extensive patient screening, certain types of physical activity (e.g., moderate vs vigorous exercise), more gradual increases in exercise, or more intensive counseling and follow-up monitoring will decrease the likelihood of injuries related to physical activity. Existing studies provide insufficient evidence regarding the potential harms of various activity protocols, such as moderate compared with vigorous exercise.

References

1. U.S. Department of Health and Human Services. *Healthy People 2010*, conference edition. Washington DC: U.S. Department of Health and Human Services; 2000. Available at: http://www.health.gov/healthypeople/ Document/HTML/Volume2/22Physical.htm. Accessed May 30, 2002.

2. U.S. Department of Health and Human Services. *Physical Activity and Health: A Report of the Surgeon General.* Atlanta, GA: U.S. Department of Health and Human Services, Centers for Disease Control and Prevention. National Center for Chronic Disease Prevention and Health Promotion; 1996. Available at: http://www.cdc.gov/nccdphp/sgr/pdf/sgrfull.pdf. Accessed May 30, 2002.

3. Task Force on Community Preventive Services. Recommendations to increase physical activity in communities. *Am J Prev Med.* 2002;22(4S):67-72. Available at: http://www.thecommunityguide.org/. Accessed June 7, 2002.

4. The Writing Group for the Activity Counseling Trial Research Group. Effects of physical activity counseling in primary care: The activity counseling trial: a randomized controlled trial. *JAMA.* 2001;286:677-687.

This USPSTF recommendation was first published in: *Ann Intern Med.* 2002;137:205-207.

Screening for Thyroid Disease

Summary of Recommendation

The U.S. Preventive Services Task Force (USPSTF) concludes the evidence is insufficient to recommend for or against routine screening for thyroid disease in adults. *Rating: I Recommendation.*

Clinical Considerations

■ Subclinical thyroid dysfunction is defined as an abnormal biochemical measurement of thyroid hormones without any specific clinical signs or symptoms of thyroid disease and no history of thyroid dysfunction or therapy. This includes individuals who have mildly elevated TSH and normal thyroxine (T4) and triiodothyronine (T3) levels (subclinical hypothyroidism), or low TSH and normal T4 and T3 levels (subclinical hyperthyroidism). Individuals with symptoms of thyroid dysfunction, or those with a history of thyroid disease or treatment, are excluded from this definition and are not the subject of these recommendations.

■ When used to confirm suspected thyroid disease in patients referred to a specialty endocrine clinic, TSH has a high sensitivity (98%) and specificity (92%). When used for screening primary care populations, the positive predictive value (PPV) of TSH in detecting thyroid disease is low; further, the interpretation of a positive test result is often complicated by an underlying illness or by frailty of the individual. In general, values for serum TSH below 0.1 mU/L are considered low and values above 6.5 mU/L are considered elevated.

■ Clinicians should be aware of subtle signs of thyroid dysfunction, particularly among those at high risk. People at higher risk for thyroid dysfunction include the elderly, post-partum women, those with high levels of radiation exposure (>20 mGy), and patients with Down syndrome. Evaluating for symptoms of hypothyroidism is difficult in patients with Down syndrome because some symptoms and signs (e.g., slow speech, thick tongue, and slow mentation) are typical findings in both conditions.

■ Subclinical hyperthyroidism has been associated with atrial fibrillation, dementia, and, less clearly, with osteoporosis. However, progression from subclinical to clinical disease in patients without a history of thyroid disease is not clearly established.

■ Subclinical hypothyroidism is associated with poor obstetric outcomes and poor cognitive development in children. Evidence for dyslipidemia, atherosclerosis, and decreased quality of life in adults with subclinical hypothyroidism in the general population is inconsistent and less convincing.

This USPSTF recommendation was first published in: *Ann Intern Med.* 2004;125-127.

Screening for Type 2 Diabetes Mellitus in Adults

Summary of Recommendations

The U.S. Preventive Services Task Force (USPSTF) concludes that the evidence is insufficient to recommend for or against routinely screening asymptomatic adults for type 2 diabetes, impaired glucose tolerance, or impaired fasting glucose. *Rating: I Recommendation.*

The USPSTF recommends screening for type 2 diabetes in adults with hypertension or hyperlipidemia. *Rating: B Recommendation.*

Clinical Considerations

■ In the absence of evidence of direct benefits of routine screening for type 2 diabetes, the decision to screen individual patients is a matter of clinical judgment. Patients at increased risk for cardiovascular disease may benefit most from screening for type 2 diabetes, since management of cardiovascular risk factors leads to reductions in major cardiovascular events. Clinicians should assist patients in making that choice. In addition, clinicians should be alert to symptoms suggestive of diabetes (ie, polydipsia and polyuria) and test anyone with these symptoms.

■ Screening for diabetes in patients with hypertension or hyperlipidemia should be part of an integrated approach to reduce cardiovascular risk. Lower targets for blood pressure (ie, diastolic blood pressure <80 mm Hg) are beneficial for patients with diabetes and high blood pressure. The report of the Adult Treatment Panel III of the National Cholesterol Education Program recommends lower targets for low-density lipoprotein cholesterol for patients with diabetes. Attention to other risk factors such as physical inactivity, diet, and overweight is also important, both to decrease risk for heart disease and to improve glucose control.

■ Three tests have been used to screen for diabetes: fasting plasma glucose (FPG), 2-hour post-load plasma glucose (2-hour PG), and hemoglobin A1c (HbA1c). The American Diabetes Association (ADA) has recommended the FPG test (>126 mg/dL) for screening because it is easier and faster to perform, more convenient and acceptable to patients, and less expensive than other screening tests. The FPG test is more reproducible than the 2-hour PG test, has less intraindividual variation, and has similar predictive value for development of microvascular complications of diabetes. Compared with the FPG test, the 2-hour PG test may lead to more individuals being diagnosed as diabetic. HbA1c is more closely related to FPG than to 2-hour PG, but at the usual cut-points it is less sensitive in detecting lower levels of hyperglycemia. The random capillary blood glucose (CBG) test has been shown to have reasonable sensitivity (75% at a cut-point of >120 mg/dL) in detecting persons who have either an FPG level >126 mg/dL or a 2-hour PG level >200 mg/dL, if results are interpreted

153

according to age and time since last meal; however, the random blood glucose test is less well standardized for screening for diabetes.

■ The ADA recommends confirmation of a diagnosis of diabetes with a repeated FPG test on a separate day, especially for patients with borderline FPG results and patients with normal FPG levels for whom suspicion of diabetes is high. The optimal screening interval is not known. The ADA, on the basis of expert opinion, recommends an interval of every 3 years but shorter intervals in high-risk persons.

■ Regardless of whether the clinician and patient decide to screen for diabetes, patients should be encouraged to exercise, eat a healthy diet, and maintain a healthy weight, choices that may prevent or forestall the development of type 2 diabetes. More aggressive interventions to establish and maintain these behaviors should be considered for patients at increased risk for developing diabetes, such as those who are overweight, have a family history of diabetes, or have a racial or ethnic background associated with an increased risk (e.g., American Indians). Intensive programs of lifestyle modification (diet, exercise, and behavior) should also be considered for patients who have impaired fasting glucose or impaired glucose tolerance, since several large trials have demonstrated that these programs can significantly reduce the incidence of diabetes in these patients. Evidence and recommendations regarding counseling about diet, physical activity, and obesity are provided in the USPSTF evidence summaries "Counseling to Promote a Healthy Diet," "Counseling to Promote Physical Activity," and "Screening and Treatment for Obesity in Adults," available on the Agency for Healthcare Research and Quality Web site at www.preventiveservices.ahrq.gov.

This USPSTF recommendation was first published in: *Ann Intern Med.* 2003; 138:212-214.

Musculoskeletal Conditions

Primary Care Interventions to Prevent Low Back Pain in Adults

Summary of Recommendation

The U.S. Preventive Services Task Force (USPSTF) concludes that the evidence is insufficient to recommend for or against the routine use of interventions to prevent low back pain in adults in primary care settings. *Rating: I Recommendation.*

Clinical Considerations

■ Although exercise has not been shown to prevent low back pain, regular physical activity has other proven health benefits, including prevention of cardiovascular disease, hypertension, type 2 diabetes, obesity, and osteoporosis.

■ Neither lumbar supports nor back belts appear to be effective in reducing the incidence of low back pain.

■ Worksite interventions, including educational interventions, have some short-term benefit in reducing the incidence of low back pain. However, their applicability to the primary care setting is unknown.

157

■ Back schools may prevent further back injury for individuals with recurrent or chronic low back pain, but their long-term effectiveness has not been well studied.

This USPSTF recommendation was first published by: Agency for Healthcare Research and Quality, Rockville, MD. February 2004. http://www.ahrq.gov/clinic/ 3rduspstf/lowback/lowbackrs.htm.

Screening for Osteoporosis in Postmenopausal Women

Summary of Recommendations

The U.S. Preventive Services Task Force (USPSTF) recommends that women aged 65 and older be screened routinely for osteoporosis. The USPSTF recommends that routine screening begin at age 60 for women at increased risk for osteoporotic fractures (see Clinical Considerations for discussion of women at increased risk). *Rating: B Recommendation.*

The USPSTF makes no recommendation for or against routine osteoporosis screening in postmenopausal women who are younger than 60 or in women aged 60-64 who are not at increased risk for osteoporotic fractures. *Rating: C Recommendation.*

Clinical Considerations

■ Modeling analysis suggests that the absolute benefits of screening for osteoporosis among women aged 60-64 who are at increased risk for osteoporosis and fracture are comparable to those of routine screening in older women. The exact risk factors that should trigger screening in this age group are difficult to specify based on evidence. Lower body weight (weight < 70 kg) is the single best predictor of low bone mineral density.[1,2] Low weight and no current use of estrogen therapy are incorporated with age into the 3-item Osteoporosis Risk Assessment Instrument (ORAI).[1,2] There is less evidence to support the use of other individual risk factors (for example, smoking, weight loss, family history, decreased physical activity, alcohol or caffeine use, or low calcium and vitamin D intake) as a basis for identifying high-risk women younger than 65. At any given age, African-American women on average have higher bone mineral density (BMD) than white women and are thus less likely to benefit from screening.

■ Among different bone measurement tests performed at various anatomical sites, bone density measured at the femoral neck by dual-energy x-ray absorptiometry (DXA) is the best predictor of hip fracture and is comparable to forearm measurements for predicting fractures at other sites. Other technologies for measuring peripheral sites include quantitative ultrasonography (QUS), radiographic absorptiometry, single energy x-ray absorptiometry, peripheral dual-energy x-ray absorptiometry, and peripheral quantitative computed tomography. Recent data suggest that peripheral bone density testing in the primary care setting can also identify postmenopausal women who have a higher risk for fracture over the short term (1 year). Further research is needed to determine the accuracy of peripheral bone density testing in comparison with dual-energy x-ray absorptiometry (DXA). The likelihood of being diagnosed with osteoporosis varies greatly depending on the site and type of bone measurement test, the number of sites tested, the brand of densitometer used, and the relevance of the reference range.

■ Estimates of the benefits of detecting and treating osteoporosis are based largely on studies of bisphosphonates. Some women, however, may prefer other treatment options (for example, hormone replacement therapy, selective estrogen receptor modulators, or calcitonin) based on personal preferences or risk factors. Clinicians should review with patients the relative benefits and harms of available treatment options, and uncertainties about their efficacy and safety, to facilitate an informed choice.

■ No studies have evaluated the optimal intervals for repeated screening. Because of limitations in the precision of testing, a minimum of 2 years may be needed to reliably measure a change in bone mineral density; however, longer intervals may be adequate for repeated screening to identify new cases of osteoporosis. Yield of repeated screening will be higher in older women, those with lower BMD at baseline, and those with other risk factors for fracture.

■ There are no data to determine the appropriate age to stop screening and few data on osteoporosis treatment in women older than 85. Patients who receive a diagnosis of osteoporosis fall outside the context of screening but may require additional testing for diagnostic purposes or to monitor response to treatment.

References

1. Cadarette SM, Jaglal SB, Kreiger N, et al. Development and validation of the Osteoporosis Risk Assessment Instrument to facilitate selection of women for bone densitometry. *Can Med Assoc J.* 2000;162:1289-1294.

2. Cadarette SM, Jaglal SB, Murray T, et al. Evaluation of decision rules for referring women for bone densitometry by dual-energy x-ray absorptiometry. *JAMA.* 2001;286(1):57-63.

This USPSTF recommendation was first published in: *Ann Intern Med.* 2002;137:526-528.

Obstetric and Gynecologic Conditions

Screening for Bacterial Vaginosis in Pregnancy

Summary of Recommendations

The U.S. Preventive Services Task Force (USPSTF) concludes that the evidence is insufficient to recommend for or against routinely screening high-risk pregnant women for bacterial vaginosis (BV). (See Clinical Considerations for discussion of populations at high risk.) *Rating: I Recommendation.*

The USPSTF recommends against routinely screening average-risk asymptomatic pregnant women for BV. *Rating: D Recommendation.*

Clinical Considerations

- For women with a history of preterm delivery, screening for BV is an option. A single previous episode of preterm delivery by itself may not reliably identify a population of women who will benefit from screening and treatment. Nevertheless, screening may be appropriate in specific circumstances. Studies demonstrating a benefit of screening and treatment were performed among populations of women at especially high risk (35% to 57%) of preterm birth. Clinicians should consider previous history of preterm delivery, other risk factors, and time of presentation in making the decision whether or not to screen for BV in women at high risk.

■ For clinicians electing to screen high-risk women, the optimal screening test is not certain. Accepted clinical criteria for BV include vaginal pH >4.5, amine odor on the application of KOH, appearance of a homogeneous vaginal discharge, and presence of clue cells on a microscopic examination of a wet mount. Presence of at least 3 of these 4 criteria is generally considered diagnostic of BV. The use of more limited criteria (e.g., clue cells alone) has not been evaluated.

■ Neither the optimal time to screen high-risk pregnant women nor the optimal treatment regimen for pregnant women with BV is clear. The 3 trials that demonstrated a reduction in preterm birth screened in the second trimester (13 to 24 weeks of pregnancy) used various regimens of oral metronidazole alone or oral metronidazole and erythromycin.

■ Treatment is appropriate for pregnant women with symptomatic BV infection. These women were excluded from most screening trials and may be at higher risk than those without symptoms. Treatment can relieve symptoms such as vaginal discharge.

This USPSTF recommendation was first published in: *Am J Prev Med.* 2001;20(3S):59-61.

Behavioral Interventions to Promote Breastfeeding

Summary of Recommendations

The U.S. Preventive Services Task Force (USPSTF) recommends structured breastfeeding education and behavioral counseling programs to promote breastfeeding. *Rating: B Recommendation.*

The USPSTF found insufficient evidence to recommend for or against the following interventions to promote breastfeeding: brief education and counseling by primary care providers; peer counseling used alone and initiated in the clinical setting; and written materials, used alone or in combination with other interventions. *Rating: I Recommendation.*

Clinical Considerations

■ Effective breastfeeding education and behavioral counseling programs use individual or group sessions led by specially trained nurses or lactation specialists, usually lasting 30 to 90 minutes. Sessions generally begin during the prenatal period and cover the benefits of breastfeeding for infant and mother, basic physiology, equipment, technical training in positioning and latch-on techniques, and behavioral training in skills required to overcome common situational barriers to breastfeeding and to garner needed social support.

■ Hospital practices that may help support breastfeeding include early maternal contact with the newborn, rooming-in, and avoidance of formula supplementation for breastfeeding infants.

■ Commercial discharge packs provided by hospitals that include samples of infant formula and/or bottles and nipples are associated with reducing the rates of exclusive breastfeeding.

■ Mothers who wish to continue breastfeeding after returning to work, especially those working full-time, may need to use an electric or mechanical pump to maintain a sufficient breast milk supply.

■ Few contraindications to breastfeeding exist. In developed countries, infection with human immunodeficiency virus (HIV) in the mother is considered a contraindication to breastfeeding, as is the presence of current alcohol and drug use/dependence. Some medications (prescription and non-prescription) are contraindicated or advised for use "with caution" and appropriate clinical monitoring among lactating women.[1] Clinicians should consult appropriate references for information on specific medications, including herbal remedies.

Reference

1. American Academy of Pediatrics and American College of Obstetricians and Gynecologists. *Guidelines for Perinatal Care,* 5th ed. October 2002:220-229.

This USPSTF recommendation was first published in: *Am J Fam Med.* 2003;1(2):79-80.

Screening for Gestational Diabetes Mellitus

Summary of Recommendation

The U.S. Preventive Services Task Force (USPSTF) concludes that the evidence is insufficient to recommend for or against routine screening for gestational diabetes. *Rating: I Recommendation.*

Clinical Considerations

■ Better quality evidence is needed to determine whether the benefits of screening for gestational diabetes mellitus (GDM) outweigh the harms. Until such evidence is available, clinicians might reasonably choose either not to screen at all or to screen only women at increased risk for GDM.

■ Patient characteristics most strongly associated with increased risk for GDM include maternal obesity (usually defined as a body mass index [BMI] of 25 or more), older age (usually defined as older than 25 years), family or personal history of diabetes, or a history of GDM in a prior pregnancy. Expert groups have also identified certain ethnic groups as being at increased risk for GDM (such as Hispanic, African American, American Indian, and South or East Asian). Using all the above criteria, however, would identify 90 percent of all pregnant women as being at increased risk for GDM.

■ The optimal approach to screening and diagnosis is uncertain. Expert panels in the United States recommend a 50-g 1-hour glucose challenge test (GCT) at 24 to 28 weeks' gestation, followed by a 100-g 3-hour oral glucose tolerance test (OGTT) for women who screen positive on the GCT. Different screening and diagnostic strategies recommended by the World Health Organization (WHO) are commonly used outside of North America. The American Diabetes Association (ADA) and the WHO have published specific criteria for diagnosis, but the USPSTF could not determine the relative benefits of any specific approach.[1,2]

References

1. WHO Consultation: Definition, diagnosis and classification of diabetes mellitus and its complications: report of a WHO Consultation. Part 1: diagnosis and classification of diabetes mellitus. Geneva, WHO/NCD/NCS/99.2, World Health Org., 1999.

2. American Diabetes Association. Gestational diabetes mellitus. *Diabetes Care.* 2002;25(Suppl 1):S94-S96.

This USPSTF recommendation was first published in: *Obstet Gynecol.* 2003;101:393-395.

Screening for Rh (D) Incompatibility

Summary of Recommendations

The U.S. Preventive Services Task Force (USPSTF) strongly recommends Rh (D) blood typing and antibody testing for all pregnant women during their first visit for pregnancy-related care. *Rating: A Recommendation.*

The USPSTF recommends repeated Rh (D) antibody testing for all unsensitized Rh (D)-negative women at 24-28 weeks' gestation, unless the biological father is known to be Rh (D)-negative. *Rating: B Recommendation.*

Clinical Considerations

■ Administration of a full (300μg) dose of Rh (D) immunoglobulin is recommended for all unsensitized Rh (D)-negative women after repeated antibody testing at 24-28 weeks' gestation.

■ If an Rh (D)-positive or weakly Rh (D)-positive (e.g., D^u-positive) infant is delivered, a dose of Rh (D) immunoglobulin should be repeated postpartum, preferably within 72 hours after delivery. Administering Rh (D) immunoglobulin at other intervals after delivery has not been studied.

■ Unless the biological father is known to be Rh (D)-negative, a full dose of Rh (D) immunoglobulin is recommended for all unsensitized Rh (D)-negative women after amniocentesis and after induced or spontaneous abortion; however, if the pregnancy is less than 13 weeks, a 50 μg dose is sufficient.

■ The benefit of routine administration of Rh (D) immunoglobulin after other obstetric procedures or complications such as chorionic villus sampling, ectopic pregnancy termination, cordocentesis, fetal surgery or manipulation (including external version), antepartum placental hemorrhage, abdominal trauma, antepartum fetal death, or stillbirth is uncertain due to inadequate evidence.

This USPSTF recommendation was first published by: Agency for Healthcare Research and Quality, Rockville, MD. February 2004. http://www.ahrq.gov/clinic/ 3rduspstf/rh/rhrs.htm.

Vision Disorders

Screening for Glaucoma

Summary of Recommendation

The U.S. Preventive Services Task Force (USPSTF) found insufficient evidence to recommend for or against screening adults for glaucoma. *Rating: I Recommendation.*

Clinical Considerations

■ Primary open angle glaucoma (POAG) is a chronic condition characterized by a loss of retinal ganglion cell axons. It is manifested initially by peripheral visual field loss; in an uncertain number of cases, it progresses to impairment in important vision-related function and even to irreversible blindness.

■ The diagnosis of POAG is not made on the basis of a single test but on the finding of characteristic degenerative changes in the optic disc and defects in visual fields. Although increased intraocular pressure (IOP) has previously been considered an important part in the definition of this condition, it is now known that many people with POAG do not have increased IOP; hence, there is little value of using tonometry to screen for POAG.

■ Increased IOP, family history, older age, and being
of African American descent place an individual at
increased risk for glaucoma. Older African
Americans have a higher prevalence of glaucoma
and perhaps a more rapid disease progression, and if
it is shown that screening for glaucoma reduces the
development of visual impairment, African
Americans would likely have greater absolute
benefit than whites. People with a limited life
expectancy would likely have little to gain from
glaucoma screening.

■ The natural history of glaucoma is heterogeneous
and not well defined. There is a subgroup of people
with POAG in whom there is either no disease
progression, or the progression is so slow that the
condition would never have an important effect on
their vision. The size of this subgroup is uncertain
and may depend on the ethnicity and age of the
population. Others experience more rapidly
progressing disease, leading to reduced vision-
related function within 10 years. Whether an
individual's glaucoma will progress cannot be
predicted with precision, but those with higher
levels of IOP and worse visual fields at baseline, and
those who are older, tend to be at greater risk for
the more rapid progression of glaucoma. Whether
the rate of progression of visual field defects remains
uniform throughout the course of glaucoma is
unknown.

■ Measurement of visual fields can be difficult. The reliability of a single visual field measurement may be low; several consistent visual field measurements are needed to establish the presence of defects. Dilated opthalmoscopy or slit lamp exam are used by specialists to examine changes in the optic disc; however, even experts vary in their ability to detect glaucomatous optic disc progression. Additionally, there is no agreed-upon single standard to define and measure progression of visual field defects.

The primary treatments for POAG reduce IOP; these include medications, laser therapy, or surgery. These treatments effectively reduce the development and progression of small, visual field defects. The magnitude of their effectiveness, however, in reducing impairment in vision-related function is uncertain. Harms caused by these interventions include formation of cataracts, harms resulting from cataract surgery, and harms of topical medication.

This USPSTF recommendation was first published by: Agency for Healthcare Research and Quality. Rockville, MD, March 2005. http://www.ahrq.gov/clinic/uspstf/uspsglau.htm.

Section 3.

Recommendations for Children

All recommendation statements in this Guide are abridged. To see the full recommendation statements and recommendations published after 2006, go to http://www.ahrq.gov/clinic/uspstf/uspstopics.htm.

Screening for Elevated Blood Lead Levels in Children and Pregnant Women

Summary of Recommendations

The U.S. Preventive Services Task Force (USPSTF) concludes that evidence is insufficient to recommend for or against routine screening for elevated blood lead levels in asymptomatic children aged 1 to 5 who are at increased risk. *Rating: I Recommendation.*

The USPSTF recommends against routine screening for elevated blood lead levels in asymptomatic children aged 1 to 5 years who are at average risk. *Rating: D Recommendation.*

The USPSTF recommends against routine screening for elevated blood lead levels in asymptomatic pregnant women. *Rating: D Recommendation.*

Clinical Considerations

- This USPSTF recommendation addresses screening for elevated blood levels in children aged 1 to 5 years who are both at average and increased risk, and in asymptomatic pregnant women.

- The highest mean blood lead levels in the U.S. occur in children aged 1-5 years (geometric mean 1.9 μg/dL). Children under 5 years of age are at greater risk for elevated blood lead levels and lead toxicity because of increased hand-to-mouth activity, increased lead absorption from the gastrointestinal tract, and the greater vulnerability of the developing central nervous system. Risk factors for increased blood lead levels in children and adults include: minority race/ethnicity; urban residence; low income; low educational attainment; older (pre-1950) housing; recent or ongoing home renovation or remodeling; pica exposure; use of ethnic remedies, certain cosmetics, and exposure to lead-glazed pottery; occupational and para-occupational exposures; and recent immigration. Additional risk factors for pregnant women include alcohol use, smoking, pica, and recent immigration status.

■ Blood lead levels in childhood, after peaking at about 2 years of age, decrease during short- and long-term followup without intervention. Most lead is stored in bone. High bone lead levels can be present with normal blood lead levels, so that blood lead levels often do not reflect the total amount of lead in the body. This could explain the lack of effect of blood lead level-lowering measures on reducing neurotoxic effects.

■ Screening tests for elevated blood lead levels include free erythrocyte (or zinc) protoporphyrin levels and capillary or venous blood lead levels. Erythrocyte (or zinc) protoporphyrin is insensitive to modest elevations in blood lead levels and lacks specificity. Blood lead concentration is more sensitive than erythrocyte protoporphyrin for detecting modest lead exposure, but its accuracy, precision, and reliability can be affected by environmental lead contamination. Therefore, venous blood lead level testing is preferred to capillary sampling. Screening questionnaires may be of value in identifying children at risk for elevated blood lead levels but should be tailored for and validated in specific communities for clinical use.

■ Treatment options in use for elevated blood lead levels include residential lead hazard-control efforts (i.e., counseling and education, dust or paint removal, and soil abatement), chelation, and nutritional interventions. In most settings, education and counseling is offered for children with blood lead levels from 10 to 20 µg/dL. Some experts have also recommended nutritional counseling for children with blood lead levels in this range. Residential lead hazard control is usually offered to children with blood lead levels ≥20 µg/dL, while chelation therapy is offered to children with blood lead levels ≥45 µg/dL.

■ Community-based interventions for the primary prevention of lead exposure are likely to be more effective, and may be more cost-effective, than office-based screening, treatment, and counseling. Relocating children who do not yet have elevated blood lead levels but who live in settings with high lead exposure may be especially helpful.

Community, regional, and national environmental lead hazard reduction efforts, such as reducing lead in industrial emissions, gasoline, and cans, have proven highly effective in reducing population blood lead levels.

This USPSTF recommendation was first published in: *Pediatrics.* 2006;118:e2514-2518.

Prevention of Dental Caries in Preschool Children

Summary of Recommendations

The U.S. Preventive Services Task Force (USPSTF) recommends that primary care clinicians prescribe oral fluoride supplementation at currently recommended doses to preschool children older than 6 months of age whose primary water source is deficient in fluoride. *Rating: B Recommendation.*

The USPSTF concludes that the evidence is insufficient to recommend for or against routine risk assessment of preschool children by primary care clinicians for the prevention of dental disease. *Rating: I Recommendation.*

Clinical Considerations

■ Dental disease is prevalent among young children, particularly those from lower socioeconomic populations; however, few preschool-aged children ever visit a dentist. Primary care clinicians are often the first and only health professionals whom children visit. Therefore, they are in a unique position to address dental disease in these children.

■ Fluoride varnishes, professionally applied topical fluorides approved to prevent dental caries in young children, are adjuncts to oral supplementation. Their advantages over other topical fluoride agents

185

(mouth-rinse and gel) include ease of use, patient acceptance, and reduced potential for toxicity.

■ Dental fluorosis (rather than skeletal fluorosis) is the most common harm of either oral fluoride or fluoride toothpaste use in children younger than 2 years in the United States. Dental fluorosis is typically very mild and only of aesthetic importance. The recommended dosage of fluoride supplementation was reduced by the American Dental Association in 1994, which is likely to decrease the prevalence and severity of dental fluorosis. The current dosage recommendations are based on the fluoride level of the local community's water supply and are available online at www.ada.org. The primary care clinician's knowledge of the fluoride level of his or her patients' primary water supply ensures appropriate fluoride supplementation and minimizes risk for fluorosis.

This USPSTF recommendation was first published in: *Am J Prev Med.* 2004;26(4)326-329.

Screening for Developmental Dysplasia of the Hip

Summary of Recommendation

The USPSTF concludes that evidence is insufficient to recommend routine screening for developmental dysplasia of the hip in infants as a means to prevent adverse outcomes. *Rating: I Recommendation.*

Clinical Considerations

■ This USPSTF screening recommendation applies only to infants who do not have obvious hip dislocations or other abnormalities evident without screening. DDH represents a spectrum of anatomic abnormalities in which the femoral head and the acetabulum are aligned improperly or grow abnormally. DDH can lead to premature degenerative joint disease, impaired walking, and pain. Risk factors for DDH include female gender, family history of DDH, breech positioning, and in utero postural deformities. However, the majority of cases of DDH have no identifiable risk factors.

■ Screening tests for DDH have limited accuracy. The most common methods of screening are serial physical examinations of the hip and lower extremities, using the Barlow and Ortolani procedures, and ultrasonography. The Barlow examination is performed by adducting a flexed hip with gentle posterior force to identify a dislocatable hip. The Ortolani examination is performed by abducting a flexed hip with gentle anterior force to relocate a dislocated hip. Data assessing the relative value of limited hip abduction as a screening tool are sparse and suggest the test is of little value in early infancy and is of somewhat greater value as infants age.

■ Treatments for DDH include both nonsurgical and surgical options. Nonsurgical treatment with abduction devices is used in early treatment and includes the commonly prescribed Pavlik method. Surgical intervention is used when DDH is severe or diagnosed late or after an unsuccessful trial of nonsurgical treatments. Evidence of the effectiveness of interventions is inconclusive because of a high rate of spontaneous resolution, absence of comparative studies of intervention versus nonintervention groups, and variations in surgical indications and protocols. Avascular necrosis of the hip is the most common and most severe potential harm of both surgical and nonsurgical interventions and can result in growth arrest of the hip and eventual joint destruction with significant disability.

References

1. Lehmann HP, Hinton R, Morello P, Santoli J. Developmental dysplasia of the hip practice guideline: technical report. Committee on Quality Improvement, and Subcommittee on Developmental Dysplasia of the Hip. *Pediatrics*. 2000;105(4):E57.

2. Bialik V, Bialik GM, Blazer S, Sujov P, Wiener F, Berant M. Developmental dysplasia of the hip: a new approach to incidence. *Pediatrics.* 1999;103(1):98-99.

3. Barlow T. Early diagnosis and treatment of congenital dislocation of the hip. *J Bone and Joint Surgery.* 1962;44:292-301.

4. Standing Medical Advisory Committee. Screening for the detection of congenital dislocation of the hip. *Arch Dis Child.* 1986;61(9):921-926.

5. Cashman JP, Round J, Taylor G, Clarke NM. The natural history of developmental dysplasia of the hip after early supervised treatment in the Pavlik harness. A prospective, longitudinal followup. *J Bone Joint Surg Br.* 2002;84(3):418-425.

6. Konigsberg DE, Karol LA, Colby S, O'Brien S. Results of medial open reduction of the hip in infants with developmental dislocation of the hip. *J Pediatr Orthop.* 2003;23(1):1-9.

This USPSTF recommendation was first published in *Pediatrics.* 2006;117:898-902.

Screening for Idiopathic Scoliosis in Adolescents

Summary of Recommendation

The U.S. Preventive Services Task Force (USPSTF) recommends against the routine screening of asymptomatic adolescents for idiopathic scoliosis. *Rating: D Recommendation.*

Clinical Considerations

- Screening adolescents for idiopathic scoliosis is usually done by visual inspection of the spine to look for asymmetry of the shoulders, scapulae, and hips. A scoliometer can be used to measure the curve. If idiopathic scoliosis is suspected, radiography can be used to confirm the diagnosis and to quantify the degree of curvature.

- The health outcomes of adolescents with idiopathic scoliosis differ from those of adolescents with secondary scoliosis (ie, congenital, neuromuscular, or early onset idiopathic scoliosis). Idiopathic scoliosis with onset in adolescence may have a milder clinical course.[1]

- Conservative interventions to treat curves detected through screening include spinal orthoses (braces) and exercise therapy, but they may not significantly improve back pain or the quality of life for adolescents diagnosed with idiopathic scoliosis.

■ The potential harms of screening and treating adolescents for idiopathic scoliosis include unnecessary follow-up visits and evaluations due to false positive test results and psychological adverse effects, especially related to brace wear. Although routine screening of adolescents for idiopathic scoliosis is not recommended, clinicians should be prepared to evaluate idiopathic scoliosis when it is discovered incidentally or when the adolescent or parent expresses concern about scoliosis.

Reference

1. Weinstein SL, Dolan LA, Spratt KF, Peterson KK, Spoonamore MJ, Ponseti IV. Health and function of patients with untreated idiopathic scoliosis: a 50-year natural history study. *JAMA.* 2003;289(5):559-567.

This USPSTF recommendation was first published by: Agency for Healthcare Research and Quality, Rockville, MD. June 2004. http://www.ahrq.gov/clinic/3rduspstf/scoliosis/scoliors.htm.

Newborn Hearing Screening

Summary of Recommendation

The U.S. Preventive Services Task Force (USPSTF) concludes the evidence is insufficient to recommend for or against routine screening of newborns for hearing loss during the postpartum hospitalization. *Rating: I Recommendation.*

Clinical Considerations

■ Currently, universal newborn hearing screening (UNHS) is required by law in more than 30 States and is performed routinely in some health care systems in other States. Selective screening of infants in the NICU and those with other risk factors for hearing loss (see below) is conducted in many settings that do not follow a policy of universal screening. Clinicians should be aware of such screening policies in their practice environments.

■ Risk factors for sensorineural hearing loss (SNHL) among newborns include NICU admission for 2 days or more; syndromes known to include hearing loss (e.g., Usher's syndrome, Waardenburg's syndrome); family history of childhood SNHL; congenital infections (e.g., toxoplasmosis, bacterial meningitis, syphilis, rubella, cytomegalovirus, herpes virus); and craniofacial abnormalities (especially morphologic abnormalities of the pinna and ear canal).

- If a program for routine hearing screening of newborns is implemented, it should include systematic education to fully inform parents and clinicians about the potential benefits and harms of the testing protocol. Most infants with positive in-hospital screening tests will subsequently be found to have normal hearing, and clinicians should be prepared to provide reassurance and support to parents of infants who need follow-up audiologic evaluation.

- If any program for newborn hearing screening is implemented, screening should be conducted using a validated protocol, usually requiring 2 screening tests. Equipment used should be well maintained, staff should be thoroughly trained, and quality control programs to reduce avoidable false-positive tests should be in place. Programs should develop protocols to ensure that infants with positive screening tests receive appropriate audiologic evaluation and follow-up after discharge.

This USPSTF recommendation was first published by: Agency for Healthcare Research and Quality, Rockville, MD. October 2001. http://www.ahrq.gov/clinic/3rduspstf/newbornscreen/newhearrr.htm.

193

Screening and Interventions for Overweight in Children and Adolescents

Summary of Recommendation

The U.S. Preventive Services Task Force (USPSTF) concludes that the evidence is insufficient to recommend for or against routine screening for overweight in children and adolescents as a means to prevent adverse health outcomes. *Rating: I Recommendation.*

Clinical Considerations

■ It is important to measure and monitor growth over time in all children as an indicator of health and development. The number of children and adolescents who are overweight has more than doubled since the early 1970s, with the prevalence of overweight (BMI > 95th percentile for age and sex) for children aged 6 to 19 years now at approximately 15 percent. The conclusion that there is insufficient evidence to recommend for or against screening for overweight in children and adolescents reflects the paucity of good-quality evidence on the effectiveness of interventions for this problem in the clinical setting. There is little evidence for effective, family-based or individual approaches for the treatment of overweight in children and adolescents in primary care settings. The Centers for Disease Control and Prevention's (CDC's) Guide to Community Preventive Services has identified effective population-based interventions that have been shown to increase physical activity, which may help reduce childhood overweight.

■ BMI (calculated as weight in kilograms divided by height in meters squared) percentile for age and sex is the preferred measure for detecting overweight in children and adolescents because of its feasibility, reliability, and tracking with adult obesity measures. BMI values are CDC population-based references for comparison of growth distribution to those of a larger population. Being at risk for overweight is defined as a BMI between the 85th and 94th percentile for age and sex, and overweight as a BMI at or above the 95th percentile for age and sex. Disadvantages of using BMI include the inability to distinguish increased fat mass from increased fat-free mass, and reference populations derived largely from non-Hispanic whites, potentially limiting its applicability to non-white populations. Indirect measures of body fat, such as skinfold thickness, bio-electrical impedance analysis, and waist-hip circumference, have potential for clinical practice, treatment, research, and longitudinal tracking, although there are limitations in measurement validity, reliability, and comparability between measures.

■ Childhood overweight is associated with a higher prevalence of intermediate metabolic consequences and risk factors for adverse health outcomes, such as insulin resistance, elevated blood lipids, increased blood pressure, and impaired glucose tolerance. Severe childhood overweight is associated with immediate morbidity from conditions such as slipped capital femoral epiphysis, steatohepatitis, and sleep apnea. Medical conditions new to this age group, such as type 2 diabetes mellitus, represent "adult" morbidities that are now seen more frequently among overweight adolescents. For most overweight children, however, medical complications do not become clinically apparent for decades.

This recommendation was first published in: *Pediatrics.* 2005;116(1):205-209.

Screening for Speech and Language Delay in Preschool Children

---

Summary of Recommendation

The U.S. Preventive Services Task Force (USPSTF) concludes that the evidence is insufficient to recommend for or against routine use of brief, formal screening instruments in primary care to detect speech and language delay in children up to 5 years of age. *Rating: I Recommendation.*

Clinical Considerations

- It is the responsibility of primary care clinicians to seek and address parents' concerns and children's obvious speech and language delays despite the lack of evidence to support screening with brief formal instruments. Speech and language development is considered a useful early indicator of a child's overall development and cognitive ability, and clinical and parental concerns are important modes of identifying children with speech and language delay. Early identification of children with developmental delay (lateness in achieving milestones) or developmental disabilities (chronic conditions that result from mental or physical impairments), such as marked hearing deficits, may lead to intervention and family assistance at a young age when chances for improvement may be best.

■ Specific groups of children who already have been identified as at higher than average risk for speech and language delay, including children with other medical problems such as hearing deficits or craniofacial abnormalities, are not considered in this recommendation. The results of studies of other risk factors are inconsistent, so the USPSTF was unable to develop a list of specific risk factors to guide primary care providers in selective screening. The most consistently reported risk factors, however, include a family history of speech and language delay, male gender, and perinatal factors, such as prematurity and low birth-weight. Other risk factors reported less consistently include levels of parental education, specific childhood illnesses, birth order, and larger family size.

This USPSTF recommendation was first published in *Pediatrics.* 2006;117(2):497-501.

Screening for Visual Impairment in Children Younger Than Age 5 Years

Summary of Recommendation

The U.S. Preventive Services Task Force (USPSTF) recommends screening to detect amblyopia, strabismus, and defects in visual acuity in children younger than age 5 years. *Rating: B Recommendation.*

Clinical Considerations

- The most common causes of visual impairment in children are: (1) amblyopia and its risk factors and (2) refractive error not associated with amblyopia. Amblyopia refers to reduced visual acuity without a detectable organic lesion of the eye and is usually associated with amblyogenic risk factors that interfere with normal binocular vision, such as strabismus (ocular misalignment), anisometropia (a large difference in refractive power between the 2 eyes), cataract (lens opacity), and ptosis (eyelid drooping). Refractive error not associated with amblyopia principally includes myopia (nearsightedness) and hyperopia (farsightedness); both remain correctable regardless of the age at detection.

- Various tests are used widely in the United States to identify visual defects in children, and the choice of tests is influenced by the child's age. During the first year of life, strabismus can be assessed by the cover test and the Hirschberg light reflex test.

Screening children younger than age 3 years for visual acuity is more challenging than screening older children and typically requires testing by specially trained personnel. Newer automated techniques can be used to test these children. Photoscreening can detect amblyogenic risk factors such as strabismus, significant refractive error, and media opacities; however, photoscreening cannot detect amblyopia.

- Traditional vision testing requires a cooperative, verbal child and cannot be performed reliably until ages 3 to 4 years. In children older than age 3 years, stereopsis (the ability of both eyes to function together) can be assessed with the Random Dot E test or Titmus Fly Stereotest; visual acuity can be assessed by tests such as the HOTV chart, Lea symbols, or the tumbling E. Some of these tests have better test characteristics than others.

- Based on their review of current evidence, the USPSTF was unable to determine the optimal screening tests, periodicity of screening, or technical proficiency required of the screening clinician. Based on expert opinion, the American Academy of Pediatrics (AAP) recommends the following vision screening be performed at all well-child visits for children starting in the newborn period to 3 years: ocular history, vision assessment, external inspection of the eyes and lids, ocular motility assessment, pupil examination, and red reflex examination. For children aged 3 to 5 years, the AAP recommends the aforementioned screening in addition to age-appropriate visual acuity measurement (using HOTV or tumbling E tests) and ophthalmoscopy.[1]

- The USPSTF found that early detection and treatment of amblyopia and amblyogenic risk factors can improve visual acuity. These treatments include surgery for strabismus and cataracts; use of glasses, contact lenses, or refractive surgery treatments to correct refractive error; and visual training, patching, or atropine therapy of the nonamblyopic eye to treat amblyopia.

- These recommendations do not address screening for other anatomic or pathologic entities, such as macro cornea, cataracts, retinal abnormalities, or neonatal neuroblastoma, nor do they address newer screening technologies currently under investigation.

Reference

1. American Academy of Pediatrics Committee on Practice and Ambulatory Medicine and Section on Ophthalmology, American Association of Certified Orthoptists, American Association of Pediatric Ophthalmology and Strabismus, American Academy of Ophthalmology. Eye examination in infants, children, and young adults by pediatricians: policy statement. *Pediatrics.* 2003;111(4):902-907.

This USPSTF recommendation was first published in: *Ann Fam Med.* 2004;2:263-266.

Appendixes
and Index

Appendix A

How the U.S. Preventive Services Task Force Grades Its Recommendations

The U.S. Preventive Services Task Force (USPSTF) grades its recommendations based on the strength of evidence and magnitude of net benefit (benefits minus harms).

A. The USPSTF strongly recommends that clinicians provide [the service] to eligible patients. *The USPSTF found good evidence that [the service] improves important health outcomes and concludes that benefits substantially outweigh harms.*

B. The USPSTF recommends that clinicians provide [the service] to eligible patients. *The USPSTF found at least fair evidence that [the service] improves important health outcomes and concludes that benefits outweigh harms.*

C. The USPSTF makes no recommendation for or against routine provision of [the service]. *The USPSTF found at least fair evidence that [the service] can improve health outcomes but concludes that the balance of benefits and harms is too close to justify a general recommendation.*

D. The USPSTF recommends against routinely providing [the service] to asymptomatic patients. *The USPSTF found at least fair evidence that [the service] is ineffective or that harms outweigh benefits.*

I. The USPSTF concludes that the evidence is insufficient to recommend for or against routinely providing [the service]. *Evidence that [the service] is effective is lacking, of poor quality, or conflicting, and the balance of benefits and harms cannot be determined.*

The USPSTF grades the quality of the overall evidence for a service on a 3-point scale (good, fair, poor).

Good: Evidence includes consistent results from well-designed, well-conducted studies in representative populations that directly assess effects on health outcomes.

Fair: Evidence is sufficient to determine effects on health outcomes, but the strength of the evidence is limited by the number, quality, or consistency of the individual studies, generalizability to routine practice, or indirect nature of the evidence on health outcomes.

Poor: Evidence is insufficient to assess the effects on health outcomes because of limited number or power of studies, important flaws in their design or conduct, gaps in the chain of evidence, or lack of information on important health outcomes.

Strength of Overall Evidence and Estimate of Net Benefit Determine the Grade.

Strength of Overall Evidence of Effectiveness	Estimate of Net Benefit (Benefit Minus Harms)			
	Substantial	Moderate	Small	Zero/Negative
Good	A	B	C	D
Fair	B	B	C	D
Poor	I – Insufficient Evidence			

Appendix B

Members of the U.S. Preventive Services Task Force 2001-2006

Janet D. Allan, Ph.D., R.N., C.S., F.A.A.N.
School of Nursing
University of Maryland, Baltimore
Baltimore, MD

Alfred O. Berg, M.D., M.P.H.
Department of Family Medicine
University of Washington
Seattle, WA

Ned Calonge, M.D., M.P.H.
Colorado Department of Public Health and Environment
Denver, CO

Thomas G. DeWitt, M.D.
Director of the Division of General and Community Pediatrics
Department of Pediatrics, Children's Hospital Medical Center
Cincinnati, OH

Paul S. Frame, M.D.
Tri-County Family Medicine
Cohocton, NY

Joxel Garcia, M.D., M.B.A.
Pan American Health Organization
Washington, DC

Leon Gordis, M.D., Dr. P.H.
Epidemiology Department
Johns Hopkins Bloomberg School of Public Health
Baltimore, MD

Kimberly D. Gregory, M.D., M.P.H.
Department of Obstetrics and Gynecology
Cedars-Sinai Medical Center
Los Angeles, CA

Russell Harris, M.D., M.P.H.
University of North Carolina School of Medicine
Chapel Hill, NC

Charles J. Homer, M.D., M.P.H.
National Initiative for Children's Healthcare Quality
Boston, MA

George Isham, M.D., M.S.
Medical Director and Chief
  Health Officer
HealthPartners
Minneapolis, MN

Mark S. Johnson, M.D., M.P.H.
Department of Family
  Medicine
New Jersey Medical School
University of Medicine and
  Dentistry of New Jersey
Newark, NJ

Kenneth Kizer, M.D., M.P.H.
National Quality Forum
Washington, DC

Jonathan D. Klein, M.D., M.P.H.
Department of Pediatrics
University of Rochester
Rochester, NY

Tracy A. Lieu, M.D., M.P.H.
Department of Ambulatory
Care and Prevention
Harvard Pilgrim Health Care
  and Harvard Medical
  School
Boston, MA

Michael L. LeFevre, M.D., M.S.P.H.
University of Missouri
School of Medicine
Columbia, MO

Carol Loveland-Cherry, Ph.D., R.N., F.A.A.N.
Office of Academic Affairs
School of Nursing,
University of Michigan
Ann Arbor, MI

Lucy N. Marion, Ph.D., R.N.
School of Nursing, Medical
College of Georgia
Augusta, GA

Virginia A. Moyer, M.D., M.P.H.
Department of Pediatrics
University of Texas Health
  Science Center
Houston, TX

Cynthia D. Mulrow, M.D., M.Sc.
University of Texas Health
  Science Center
Audie L. Murphy Memorial
  Veterans Hospital
San Antonio, TX

Judith K. Ockene, Ph.D., M.Ed.
Division of Preventive and
  Behavioral Medicine
University of Massachusetts
  Medical School
Worcester, MA

C. Tracy Orleans, Ph.D.
Department of Research and
Evaluation
The Robert Wood Johnson
Foundation
Princeton, NJ

**Jeffrey F. Peipert, M.D.,
M.P.H.**
Women and Infants'
Hospital
Providence, RI

Nola J. Pender, Ph.D., R.N.
School of Nursing
University of Michigan
Ann Arbor, MI

**Diana B. Petitti, M.D.,
M.P.H.**
Kaiser Permanente Southern
California
Pasadena, CA

George F. Sawaya, M.D.
Department of Obstetrics,
Gynecology, and
Reproductive Sciences
Department of
Epidemiology and
Biostatistics
University of California,
San Francisco
San Francisco, CA

Harold C. Sox, Jr., M.D.
Department of Medicine
Dartmouth-Hitchcock
Medical Center
Lebanon, NH

Albert L. Siu, M.D., M.S.P.H.
Brookdale Department of
Geriatrics and Adult
Development
Mount Sinai Medical Center
New York, NY

**Steven M. Teutsch, M.D.,
M.P.H.**
Merck and Company, Inc.
West Point, PA

Carolyn Westhoff, M.D., M.Sc.
Department of Obstetrics
and Gynecology
Columbia University
New York, NY

**Steven H. Woolf, M.D.,
M.P.H.**
Department of Family
Practice, Preventive
Medicine, and
Community Health
Virginia Commonwealth
University
Fairfax, VA

Barbara P. Yawn, M.D., M.Sc.
Olmstead Research Center
Rochester, MN

Appendix C

Acknowledgments

AHRQ Staff Supporting the USPSTF 2001-2006

David Atkins, M.D., M.P.H.
Mary Barton, M.D., M.P.P.
Dana Best, M.D., M.P.H.
Joel Boches
Helen Burstin, M.D., M.P.H.
Mackenzie Cross
Sandra K. Cummings
Elizabeth Edgerton, M.D., M.P.H.
Farah Englert
Kenneth Fink, M.D., M.G.A., M.P.H.
Janice L. Genevro, Ph.D., M.S.W.
Barbara Gordon
Margi Grady
Janelle Guirguis-Blake, M.D.
Patrik Johansson, M.D.
Heather Johnson
Douglas Kamerow, M.D., M.P.H.
Hazel Keimowitz, M.A.
Claire Kendrick, M.S.Ed.
David Lanier, M.D.
Kenneth Lin, M.D.
Iris Mabry, M.D., M.P.H.
Corey Mackison, M.S.A.
David Meyers, M.D.
Tess Miller, Dr.P.H.
Kevin Murray
Barbara Najar, M.P.H.
Bridget O'Connell
Nilam Patel, M.P.H.
Amy Pfeiffer
Gurvaneet Randhawa, M.D., M.P.H.
Stacia Sanvick

Eve Shapiro
Randie Siegel, M.S.
Jean Slutsky, P.A., M.S.P.H.
Kristie Smith
Marion Torchia
Tricia Trinité, M.S.P.H., A.P.R.N.
Tracy Wolff, M.D., M.P.H.

Evidence-Based Practice Centers
Supporting the USPSTF 2001-2006
The following researchers working through three AHRQ
Evidence-Based Practice Centers prepared systematic evidence
reviews and evidence summaries as resources on topics under
consideration by the USPSTF.

Oregon Evidence-Based Practice Center
Mikel Aickin, Ph.D.; Sarah Baird, M.S.; Vance Bauer, M.A.;
Tracy Beil, M.S.; Christina Bougatsos, B.S.; Jessica Burnett;
David Buckley, M.D.; Taryn Cardenas, B.S.; Susan Carson,
M.P.H.; Benjamin K.S. Chan, M.S.; Roger Chou, M.D.;
Elizabeth Clark, M.D., M.P.H; Robert Davis, M.D., M.P.H.;
Stephanie Detlefsen, M.D.; Karen B. Eden, Ph.D.; Michelle
Eder, Ph.D.; Craig Fleming, M.D.; Michele Freeman, M.P.H.;
Rochele Fu, Ph.D.; Nancy Glass, Ph.D., M.P.H., R.N.;
Rachel Gold, Ph.D., M.P.H; Carla A. Green, Ph.D., M.P.H.;
Jeanne-Marie Guise, M.D., M.P.H.; Andrew Hamilton, M.S.,
M.L.S.; Elizabeth Haney, M.D; Emily Harris, Ph.D., M.P.H.;
Mark Helfand, M.D., M.P.H.; Theresa Hillier, M.D., M.S.;
Laurie Huffman, M.S.; Linda Humphrey, M.D., M.P.H.;
Devan Kansagara, M.D.; P. Todd Korthuis, M.D., M.P.H;
Kathryn Pyle Krages, M.A.; Erin Leblanc, M.D., M.P.H.;
Beth Liles, M.D.; Jennifen Lin, M.D.; Susan Mahon, M.P.H.;
Yasmin McInerney, M.D.; Heather McPhillips, M.D.,
M.P.H.; Yvonne Michael, Sc.D.; Jill Miller, M.D.; Cynthia D.
Morris, Ph.D., M.P.H.; Cynthia Mulrow, M.D., M.Sc.;
Arpana Naik, M.D.; Heidi D. Nelson, M.D., M.P.H.;
Rebecca Newton-Thompson, M.D., M.Sc.; Susan Norris,

M.D., M.P.H.; Peggy Nygren, M.S.; Tracy Orleans, Ph.D.;
Valerie Palda, M.D., M.P.H.; Rita Panosca, M.D.; Nola
Pender, Ph.D., R.N., F.A.A.N.; , Jeffrey Piepert, M.D.,
M.P.H.; Daphne Plaut, M.L.S.; Michael R. Polen, Ph.D.;
Elizabeth O'Connor, Ph.D.; Gary Rischitelli, M.D., J.D.,
M.P.H.; Cheryl Ritenbaugh, Ph.D., M.P.H.; Kevin Rogers,
M.D.; Somnath Saha, M.D., M.P.H.; Scott A. Shipman,
M.D., M.P.H.; Paula R. Smith, R.N., B.S.N.; Ariel K. Smits,
M.D., M.P.H.; Robert Steiner, M.D.; Kelly Streit, M.S.,
R.D.; Lina M.A. Takano, M.D., M.S.; Diane Thompson,
M.S.; Kari Tyne, M.D.; Kimberly Vesco, M.D., M.P.H.; Kim
Villemyer, B.A.; Miranda Walker, B.A.; Carolyn Westoff,
M.D., M.Sc.; Evelyn P. Whitlock, M.D., M.P.H.; Selvi
B.Williams, M.D., M.P.H.; Jennifer Wisdom, Ph.D., M.P.H.;
Sarah Zuber, B.A.

RTI International/University of North Carolina Evidence-Based Practice Center

Alice Ammerman, Dr.P.H., R.D.; James D. Bader, D.D.S.,
M.P.H.; Rainer Beck, M.D.; John F. Boggess, M.D.; Malaz
Boustani, M.D., M.P.H.; Seth Brody, M.D.; Audrina J.
Bunton; Katrina Donahue, M.D., M.P.H.; Louise Fernandez,
PA-C, R.D., M.P.H.; Kenneth Fink, M.D., M.G.A., M.P.H.;
Carol Ford, M.D.; Angela Fowler-Brown, M.D.; Bradley N.
Gaynes, M.D., M.P.H.; Paul Godley, M.D., M.P.H.; Susan A.
Hall, M.S.; Laura Hanson, M.D., M.P.H.; Russell Harris,
M.D., M.P.H.; Katherine E.Hartmann, M.D., Ph.D.;
Michael Hayden, M.D.; M. Brian Hemphill, M.D.; Alissa
Driscoll Jacobs, M.S., R.D.; Jana Johnson; Linda Kinsinger,
M.D., M.P.H.; Carol Krasnov; Ramesh Krishnaraj; Carole M.
Lannon, M.D., M.P.H.; Carmen Lewis, M.D., M.P.H.;
Kathleen N. Lohr, Ph.D.; Linda J. Lux, M.P.A.; Kathleen
McTigue, M.D., M.P.H.; Catherine Mills, M.A.; Kavita
Nanda, M.D., M.H.S.; Carla Nester, M.D.; Britt Peterson,
M.D., M.P.H.; Christopher J. Phillips, M.D., M.P.H.;
Michael Pignone, M.D., M.P.H.; Mark Pletcher, M.D.,
M.P.H.; Saif S. Rathore; Melissa Rich, M.D.; Gary Rozier,

D.D.S.; Jerry L. Rushton, M.D., M.P.H.; Lucy A. Savitz; Joe Scattoloni; Stacey Sheridan, M.D., M.P.H.; Sonya Sutton, B.S.P.H.; Jeffrey A. Tice, M.D.; Suzanne L. West, Ph.D.; B. Lynn Whitener, Dr.P.H., M.S.L.S.; Margaret Wooddell, M.A.; Dennis Zolnoun, M.D.

University of Ottawa Evidence-Based Practice Center
Nicholas Barrowman, Ph.D.; Catherine Code, M.D., F.R.C.P.C.; Catherine Dubé, M.D., M.Sc., F.R.C.P.C.; Gabriela Lewin, M.D.; David Moher, Ph.D.; Alaa Rostom, M.D., M.Sc., F.R.C.P.C.; Margaret Sampson, M.I.L.S.; Alexander Tsertsvadze, M.D., M.Sc.

Liaisons to the USPSTF

Professional Organizations
American Academy of Family Physicians
American Academy of Nurse Practitioners
American Academy of Pediatrics
American Academy of Physician Assistants
American College of Obstetricians and Gynecologists
American College of Physicians
American College of Preventive Medicine
American Medical Association
American Osteopathic Association
America's Health Insurance Plans
National Organization of Nurse Practitioner Faculties

Government Agencies
Canadian Task Force on Preventive Health Care
Centers for Disease Control & Prevention
Centers for Medicare & Medicaid Services
Health Resources and Services Administration
Indian Health Services
Military Health System
National Institutes of Health
U.S. Food and Drug Administration
VA National Center for Health Promotion and Disease
  Prevention

Advisory Committee on Immunization Practices Recommended Immunization Schedules

The USPSTF recognizes the importance of immunizations in primary disease prevention. The Task Force refers to recommendations made by the Centers for Disease Control and Prevention's Advisory Committee on Immunization Practices (ACIP) for immunization of children and adults. The methods used by ACIP to review evidence on immunizations may differ from the methods used by the USPSTF.

Recommended Immunization Schedule for Persons Aged 0–6 Years—UNITED STATES · 2007

Legend:
- Range of recommended ages
- Catch-up immunization
- Certain high-risk groups

Vaccine ▼	Age ▶	Birth	1 month	2 months	4 months	6 months	12 months	15 months	18 months	19–23 months	2–3 years	4–6 years
Hepatitis B[1]		HepB	HepB			HepB				HepB Series		
Rotavirus[2]				Rota	Rota	Rota						
Diphtheria, Tetanus, Pertussis[3]				DTaP	DTaP	DTaP		DTaP				DTaP
Haemophilus influenzae type b[4]				Hib	Hib	Hib[d]	Hib					
Pneumococcal[5]				PCV	PCV	PCV	PCV				PCV / PPV	
Inactivated Poliovirus[6]				IPV	IPV	IPV						IPV
Influenza[6]						Influenza (Yearly)						
Measles, Mumps, Rubella[7]							MMR					MMR
Varicella[8]							Varicella					Varicella
Hepatitis A[9]							HepA (2 doses)				HepA Series	
Meningococcal[10]											MPSV4	

Footnotes begin on page 216.

The Recommended Immunization Schedules for Persons Aged 0–18 Years are approved by:

Advisory Committee on Immunization Practices (http://www.cdc.gov/nip/acip)

American Academy of Pediatrics (http://www.aap.org)

American Academy of Family Physicians (http://www.aafp.org)

Keep track of your child's immunizations
with the
CDC Childhood Immunization Scheduler
www.cdc.gov/nip/kidstuff/scheduler.htm

More information regarding vaccine administration can be obtained from the websites above or the CDC-INFO contact center:

800-CDC-INFO
ENGLISH & ESPAÑOL – 24/7
[800-232-4636]

DEPARTMENT OF HEALTH AND HUMAN SERVICES
CENTERS FOR DISEASE CONTROL AND PREVENTION
SAFER·HEALTHIER·PEOPLE™

This schedule indicates the recommended ages for routine administration of currently licensed childhood vaccines, as of December 1, 2006, for children aged 0–6 years. Additional information is available at **http://www.cdc.gov/nip/recs/child-schedule.htm**. Any dose not administered at the recommended age should be administered at any subsequent visit, when indicated and feasible. Additional vaccines may be licensed and recommended during the year. Licensed combination vaccines may be used whenever any components of the combination are indicated and other components of the vaccine are not contraindicated and if approved by the Food and Drug Administration for that dose of the series. Providers should consult the respective Advisory Committee on Immunization Practices statement for detailed recommendations. Clinically significant adverse events that follow immunization should be reported to the Vaccine Adverse Event Reporting System (VAERS). Guidance about how to obtain and complete a VAERS form is available at **http://www.vaers.hhs.gov** or by telephone, **800-822-7967.**

215

Footnotes

1. Hepatitis B vaccine (HepB). *(Minimum age: birth)*

At birth:

- Administer monovalent HepB to all newborns before hospital discharge.
- If mother is hepatitis surface antigen (HBsAg)-positive, administer HepB and 0.5 mL of hepatitis B immune globulin (HBIG) within 12 hours of birth.
- If mother's HBsAg status is unknown, administer HepB within 12 hours of birth. Determine the HBsAg status as soon as possible and if HBsAg-positive, administer HBIG (no later than age 1 week).
- If mother is HBsAg-negative, the birth dose can only be delayed with physician's order and mother's negative HBsAg laboratory report documented in the infant's medical record.

After the birth dose:

- The HepB series should be completed with either monovalent HepB or a combination vaccine containing HepB. The second dose should be administered at age 1–2 months. The final dose should be administered at age ≥ 24 weeks. Infants born to HBsAg-positive mothers should be tested for HBsAg and antibody to HBsAg after completion of ≥ 3 doses of a licensed HepB series, at age 9–18 months (generally at the next well-child visit).

4-month dose:

- It is permissible to administer 4 doses of HepB when combination vaccines are administered after the birth dose. If monovalent HepB is used for doses after the birth dose, a dose at age 4 months is not needed.

2. **Rotavirus vaccine (Rota).** *(Minimum age: 6 weeks)*
   - Administer the first dose at age 6–12 weeks. Do not start the series later than age 12 weeks.
   - Administer the final dose in the series by age 32 weeks. Do not administer a dose later than age 32 weeks.
   - Data on safety and efficacy outside of these age ranges are insufficient.

3. **Diphtheria and tetanus toxoids and acellular pertussis vaccine (DTaP).** *(Minimum age: 6 weeks)*
   - The fourth dose of DTaP may be administered as early as age 12 months, provided 6 months have elapsed since the third dose.
   - Administer the final dose in the series at age 4–6 years.

4. **Haemophilus influenzae type b conjugate vaccine (Hib).** *(Minimum age: 6 weeks)*
   - If PRP-OMP (PedvaxHIB® or ComVax® [Merck]) is administered at ages 2 and 4 months, a dose at age 6 months is not required.
   - TriHiBit® (DTaP/Hib) combination products should not be used for primary immunization but can be used as boosters following any Hib vaccine in children aged ≥12 months.

5. **Pneumococcal vaccine.** *(Minimum age: 6 weeks for pneumococcal conjugate vaccine [PCV]; 2 years for pneumococcal polysaccharide vaccine [PPV])*
   - Administer PCV at ages 24–59 months in certain high-risk groups. Administer PPV to children aged ≥ 2 years in certain high-risk groups. See *MMWR* 2000;49(No. RR-9):1–35.

6. **Influenza vaccine.** *(Minimum age: 6 months for trivalent inactivated influenza vaccine [TIV]; 5 years for live, attenuated influenza vaccine [LAIV])*
   - All children aged 6–59 months and close contacts of all children aged 0–59 months are recommended to receive influenza vaccine.

- Influenza vaccine is recommended annually for children aged ≥ 59 months with certain risk factors, health-care workers, and other persons (including household members) in close contact with persons in groups at high risk. See *MMWR* 2006;55(No. RR-10):1–41.
- For healthy persons aged 5–49 years, LAIV may be used as an alternative to TIV.
- Children receiving TIV should receive 0.25 mL if aged 6–35 months or 0.5 mL if aged ≥ 3 years.
- Children aged <9 years who are receiving influenza vaccine for the first time should receive 2 doses (separated by ≥ 4 weeks for TIV and ≥ 6 weeks for LAIV).

7. Measles, mumps, and rubella vaccine (MMR). *(Minimum age: 12 months)*

• Administer the second dose of MMR at age 4–6 years. MMR may be administered before age 4–6 years, provided ≥ 4 weeks have elapsed since the first dose and both doses are administered at age ≥ 12 months.

8. Varicella vaccine. *(Minimum age: 12 months)*

- Administer the second dose of varicella vaccine at age 4–6 years. Varicella vaccine may be administered before age 4–6 years, provided that ≥ 3 months have elapsed since the first dose and both doses are administered at age ≥12 months. If second dose was administered ≥ 28 days following the first dose, the second dose does not need to be repeated.

9. Hepatitis A vaccine (HepA). *(Minimum age: 12 months)*

- HepA is recommended for all children aged 1 year (i.e., aged 12–23 months). The 2 doses in the series should be administered at least 6 months apart.

- Children not fully vaccinated by age 2 years can be vaccinated at subsequent visits.
- HepA is recommended for certain other groups of children, including in areas where vaccination programs target older children. See *MMWR* 2006;55(No. RR-7):1–23.

10. Meningococcal polysaccharide vaccine (MPSV4). *(Minimum age: 2 years)*

- Administer MPSV4 to children aged 2–10 years with terminal complement deficiencies or anatomic or functional asplenia and certain other high risk groups. See *MMWR* 2005;54(No. RR-7):1–21.

Recommended Immunization Schedule for Persons Aged 7–18 Years—UNITED STATES • 2007

Vaccine ▼	Age ▶	7–10 years	11–12 YEARS	13–14 years	15 years	16–18 years
Tetanus, Diphtheria, Pertussis[1]		see footnote 1	Tdap	Tdap		
Human Papillomavirus[2]		see footnote 2	HPV (3 doses)	HPV Series		
Meningococcal[3]		MPSV4	MCV4		MCV4 / MCV4	
Pneumococcal[4]			PPV			
Influenza[5]			Influenza (Yearly)			
Hepatitis A[6]			HepA Series			
Hepatitis B[7]			HepB Series			
Inactivated Poliovirus[8]			IPV Series			
Measles, Mumps, Rubella[9]			MMR Series			
Varicella[10]			Varicella Series			

Range of recommended ages

Catch-up immunization

Certain high-risk groups

Footnotes begin on page 222.

220

This schedule indicates the recommended ages for routine administration of currently licensed childhood vaccines, as of December 1, 2006, for children aged 7–18 years. Additional information is available at http://www.cdc.gov/nip/recs/child-schedule.htm. Any dose not administered at the recommended age should be administered at any subsequent visit, when indicated and feasible.

Additional vaccines may be licensed and recommended during the year. Licensed combination vaccines may be used whenever any components of the combination are indicated and other components of the vaccine are not contraindicated and if approved by the Food and Drug Administration for that dose of the series. Providers should consult the respective Advisory Committee on Immunization Practices statement for detailed recommendations. Clinically significant adverse events that follow immunization should be reported to the Vaccine Adverse Event Reporting System (VAERS). Guidance about how to obtain and complete a VAERS form is available at **http://www.vaers.hhs.gov** or by telephone, **800-822-7967**.

Footnotes

1. **Tetanus and diphtheria toxoids and acellular pertussis vaccine (Tdap).** *(Minimum age: 10 years for BOOSTRIX® and 11 years for ADACEL™)*

   • Administer at age 11–12 years for those who have completed the recommended childhood DTP/DTaP vaccination series and have not received a tetanus and diphtheria toxoids vaccine (Td) booster dose.

   • Adolescents aged 13–18 years who missed the 11–12 year Td/Tdap booster dose should also receive a single dose of Tdap if they have completed the recommended childhood DTP/DTaP vaccination series.

2. **Human papillomavirus vaccine (HPV).** *(Minimum age: 9 years)*

   • Administer the first dose of the HPV vaccine series to females at age 11–12 years.

   • Administer the second dose 2 months after the first dose and the third dose 6 months after the first dose.

   • Administer the HPV vaccine series to females at age 13–18 years if not previously vaccinated.

3. **Meningococcal vaccine.** *(Minimum age: 11 years for meningococcal conjugate vaccine [MCV4]; 2 years for meningococcal polysaccharide vaccine [MPSV4])*

   • Administer MCV4 at age 11–12 years and to previously unvaccinated adolescents at high school entry (at approximately age 15 years).

- Administer MCV4 to previously unvaccinated college freshmen living in dormitories; MPSV4 is an acceptable alternative.

- Vaccination against invasive meningococcal disease is recommended for children and adolescents aged ≥ 2 years with terminal complement deficiencies or anatomic or functional asplenia and certain other high-risk groups. See *MMWR* 2005;54(No. RR-7):1–21. Use MPSV4 for children aged 2–10 years and MCV4 or MPSV4 for older children.

4. Pneumococcal polysaccharide vaccine (PPV). *(Minimum age: 2 years)*

- Administer for certain high-risk groups. See *MMWR* 1997;46(No. RR-8):1–24, and *MMWR* 2000;49(No. RR-9):1–35.

5. Influenza vaccine. *(Minimum age: 6 months for trivalent inactivated influenza vaccine [TIV]; 5 years for live, attenuated influenza vaccine [LAIV])*

- Influenza vaccine is recommended annually for persons with certain risk factors, health-care workers, and other persons (including household members) in close contact with persons in groups at high risk. See *MMWR* 2006;55 (No. RR-10):1–41.

- For healthy persons aged 5–49 years, LAIV may be used as an alternative to TIV.

- Children aged <9 years who are receiving influenza vaccine for the first time should receive 2 doses (separated by ≥ 4 weeks for TIV and ≥ 6 weeks for LAIV).

223

6. **Hepatitis A vaccine (Hep A).** (*Minimum age: 12 months*)

   • The 2 doses in the series should be administered at least 6 months apart.

   • HepA is recommended for certain other groups of children, including in areas where vaccination programs target older children. See *MMWR* 2006;55 (No.RR-7):1–23.

7. **Hepatitis B vaccine (Hep B).** (*Minimum age: birth*)

   • Administer the 3-dose series to those who were not previously vaccinated.

   • A 2-dose series of Recombivax HB® is licensed for children aged 11–15 years.

8. **Inactivated poliovirus vaccine (IPV).** (*Minimum age: 6 weeks*)

   • For children who received an all-IPV or all-oral poliovirus (OPV) series, a fourth dose is not necessary if the third dose was administered at age ≥ 4 years.

   • If both OPV and IPV were administered as part of a series, a total of 4 doses should be administered, regardless of the child's current age.

9. **Measles, mumps, and rubella vaccine (MMR).** (*Minimum age: 12months*)

   • If not previously vaccinated, administer 2 doses of MMR during any visit, with ≥ 4 weeks between the doses.

10. Varicella vaccine. *(Minimum age: 12 months)*

- Administer 2 doses of varicella vaccine to persons without evidence of immunity.
- Administer 2 doses of varicella vaccine to persons aged <13 years at least 3 months apart. Do not repeat the second dose, if administered ≥ 28 days after the first dose.
- Administer 2 doses of varicella vaccine to persons aged ≥ 13 years at least 4 weeks apart.

225

| | | CATCH-UP SCHEDULE FOR PERSONS AGED 4 MONTHS–6 YEARS | | | |
| Vaccine | Minimum Age for Dose 1 | Minimum Interval Between Doses | | | |
		Dose 1 to Dose 2	Dose 2 to Dose 3	Dose 3 to Dose 4	Dose 4 to Dose 5
Hepatitis B[1]	Birth	4 weeks	8 weeks (and 16 weeks after first dose)		
Rotavirus[2]	6 wks	4 weeks	4 weeks		
Diphtheria, Tetanus, Pertussis[3]	6 wks	4 weeks	4 weeks	6 months	6 months[3]
Haemophilus influenzae type b[4]	6 wks	4 weeks if first dose administered at age <12 months and current age <24 months 8 weeks (as final dose) if first dose administered at age 12–14 months No further doses needed if first dose administered at age ≥15 months	4 weeks[4] if current age <12 months 8 weeks (as final dose)[4] if current age ≥12 months and second dose administered at age <15 months No further doses needed if previous dose administered at age ≥15 months	8 weeks (as final dose) This dose only necessary for children aged 12 months–5 years who received 3 doses before age 12 months	
Pneumococcal[5]	6 wks	4 weeks if first dose administered at age <12 months and current age <24 months 8 weeks (as final dose) if first dose administered at age ≥12 months or current age 24–59 months No further doses needed for healthy children if first dose administered at age ≥24 months	4 weeks if current age <12 months 8 weeks (as final dose) if current age ≥12 months No further doses needed for healthy children if previous dose administered at age ≥24 months	8 weeks (as final dose) This dose only necessary for children aged 12 months–5 years who received 3 doses before age 12 months	
Inactivated Poliovirus[6]	6 wks	4 weeks	4 weeks	4 weeks[6]	
Measles, Mumps, Rubella[7]	12 mos	4 weeks			
Varicella[7]	12 mos	3 months			
Hepatitis A[9]	12 mos	6 months			

226

Catch-up Immunization Schedule

UNITED STATES • 2007

for Persons Aged 4 Months–18 Years Who Start Late or Who Are More Than 1 Month Behind

		CATCH-UP SCHEDULE FOR PERSONS AGED 7–18 YEARS		
Tetanus, Diphtheria/ Tetanus, Diphtheria, Pertussis[10]	7 yrs[10]	4 weeks	8 weeks if first dose administered at age <12 months 6 months if first dose administered at age ≥12 months	6 months if first dose administered at age <12 months
Human Papillomavirus[11]	9 yrs	4 weeks	12 weeks	
Hepatitis A[9]	12 mos	6 months		
Hepatitis B[1]	Birth	4 weeks	8 weeks (and 16 weeks after first dose)	
Inactivated Poliovirus[8]	6 wks	4 weeks	4 weeks	4 weeks[6]
Measles, Mumps, Rubella[7]	12 mos	4 weeks		
Varicella[8]	12 mos	4 weeks if first dose administered at age ≥13 years 3 months if first dose administered at age <13 years		

Footnotes begin on page 228.

This table provides catch-up schedules and minimum intervals between doses for children whose vaccinations have been delayed. A vaccine series does not need to be restarted, regardless of the time that has elapsed between doses. Use the section appropriate for the child's age.

Footnotes

1. Hepatitis B vaccine (HepB). *(Minimum age: birth)*

- Administer the 3-dose series to those who were not previously vaccinated.
- A 2-dose series of Recombivax HIB® is licensed for children aged 11–15 years.

2. Rotavirus vaccine (Rota). *(Minimum age: 6 weeks)*

- Do not start the series later than age 12 weeks.
- Administer the final dose in the series by age 32 weeks. Do not administer a dose later than age 32 weeks.
- Data on safety and efficacy outside of these age ranges are insufficient.

3. Diphtheria and tetanus toxoids and acellular pertussis vaccine (DTaP). *(Minimum age: 6 weeks)*

- The fifth dose is not necessary if the fourth dose was administered at age ≥ 4 years.
- DTaP is not indicated for persons aged ≥ 7 years.

4. Haemophilus influenzae type b conjugate vaccine (Hib). *(Minimum age: 6 weeks)*

- Vaccine is not generally recommended for children aged ≥ 5 years.
- If current age <12 months and the first 2 doses were PRP-OMP (PedvaxHIB® or ComVax® [Merck]), the third (and final) dose should be administered at age 12–15 months and at least 8 weeks after the second dose.

- If first dose was administered at age 7–11 months, administer 2 doses separated by 4 weeks plus a booster at age 12–15 months.

5. Pneumococcal conjugate vaccine (PCV). *(Minimum age: 6 weeks)*

- Vaccine is not generally recommended for children aged ≥ 5 years.

6. Inactivated poliovirus vaccine (IPV). *(Minimum age: 6 weeks)*

- For children who received an all-IPV or all-oral poliovirus (OPV) series, a fourth dose is not necessary if third dose was administered at age ≥ 4 years.

- If both OPV and IPV were administered as part of a series, a total of 4 doses should be administered, regardless of the child's current age.

7. Measles, mumps, and rubella vaccine (MMR). *(Minimum age: 12 months)*

- The second dose of MMR is recommended routinely at age 4–6 years but may be administered earlier if desired.

- If not previously vaccinated, administer 2 doses of MMR during any visit with ≥ 4 weeks between the doses.

8. Varicella vaccine. *(Minimum age: 12 months)*

- The second dose of varicella vaccine is recommended routinely at age 4–6 years but may be administered earlier if desired.

- Do not repeat the second dose in persons aged <13 years if administered ≥ 28 days after the first dose.

9. Hepatitis A vaccine (HepA). *(Minimum age: 12 months)*

- HepA is recommended for certain groups of children, including in areas where vaccination programs target older children. See *MMWR* 2006;55(No. RR-7):1–23.

10. Tetanus and diphtheria toxoids vaccine (Td) and tetanus and diphtheria toxoids and acellular pertussis vaccine (Tdap). *(Minimum ages: 7 years for Td, 10 years for BOOSTRIX®, and 11 years for ADACEL™)*

- Tdap should be substituted for a single dose of Td in the primary catch-up series or as a booster if age appropriate; use Td for other doses.
- A 5-year interval from the last Td dose is encouraged when Tdap is used as a booster dose. A booster (fourth) dose is needed if any of the previous doses were administered at age <12 months. Refer to ACIP recommendations for further information. See *MMWR* 2006;55(No. RR-3).

11. Human papillomavirus vaccine (HPV). *(Minimum age: 9 years)*

- Administer the HPV vaccine series to females at age 13–18 years if not previously vaccinated.

Information about reporting reactions after immunization is available online at **http://www.vaers.hhs.gov** or by telephone via the 24-hour national toll-free information line 800-822-7967. Suspected cases of vaccine-preventable diseases should be reported to the State or local health department. Additional information, including precautions and contraindications for immunization, is available from the National Center for Immunization and Respiratory Diseases at **http://www.cdc.gov/vaccines/** or telephone, **800-CDC-INFO** (**800-232-4636**).

Recommended Adult Immunization Schedule, by Vaccine and Age Group
UNITED STATES • OCTOBER 2006–SEPTEMBER 2007

Vaccine ▼ Age group ▶	19—49 years	50—64 years	≥65 years
Tetanus, diphtheria, pertussis (Td/Tdap)*	Substitute 1 dose of Tdap for Td	1-dose Td booster every 10 yrs	
Human papillomavirus (HPV)	3 doses (females)		
Measles, mumps, rubella (MMR)*	1 or 2 doses	1 dose	
Varicella*	2 doses (0, 4–8 wks)	2 doses (0, 4–8 wks)	
Influenza*	1 dose annually	1 dose annually	
Pneumococcal (polysaccharide)	1–2 doses		1 dose
Hepatitis A*	2 doses (0, 6–12 mos, or 0, 6–18 mos)		
Hepatitis B*	3 doses (0, 1–2, 4–6 mos)		
Meningococcal	1 or more doses		

*Covered by the Vaccine Injury Compensation Program. NOTE: This schedule should be read along with the footnotes, which can be found at www.cdc.gov/nip/recs/adult-schedule.htm.

For all persons in this category who meet the age requirements and who lack evidence of immunity (e.g., lack documentation of vaccination or have no evidence of prior infection)

Recommended if some other risk factor is present (e.g., on the basis of medical, occupational, lifestyle, or other indications)

232

Approved by
the Advisory Committee on
Immunization Practices,
the American College of Obstetricians
and Gynecologists,
the American Academy of
Family Physicians,
and the American College of
Physicians

DEPARTMENT OF HEALTH AND HUMAN SERVICES
CENTERS FOR DISEASE CONTROL AND PREVENTION

This schedule indicates the recommended age groups and medical indications for routine administration of currently licensed vaccines for persons aged ≥19 years, as of October 1, 2006. Licensed combination vaccines may be used whenever any components of the combination are indicated and when the vaccine's other components are not contraindicated. For detailed recommendations on all vaccines, including those used primarily for travelers or that are issued during the year, consult the manufacturers' package inserts and the complete statements from the Advisory Committee on Immunization Practices (www.cdc.gov/nip/publications/acip-list.htm).

Report all clinically significant postvaccination reactions to the Vaccine Adverse Event Reporting System (VAERS). Reporting forms and instructions on filing a VAERS report are available at www.vaers.hhs.gov or by telephone, 800-822-7967.

Information on how to file a Vaccine Injury Compensation Program claim is available at www.hrsa.gov/vaccinecompensation or by telephone, 800-338-2382. To file a claim for vaccine injury, contact the U.S. Court of Federal Claims, 717 Madison Place, N.W., Washington, D.C. 20005; telephone, 202-357-6400.

Additional information about the vaccines in this schedule and contraindications for vaccination is also available at www.cdc.gov/nip or from the CDC-INFO Contact Center at 800-CDC-INFO (800-232-4636) in English and Spanish, 24 hours a day, 7 days a week.

Recommended Adult Immunization Schedule, by Vaccine and Medical and Other Indications
UNITED STATES • OCTOBER 2006–SEPTEMBER 2007

Vaccine ▼ / Indication ▶	Pregnancy	Congenital immunodeficiencies, leukemia, lymphoma, generalized malignancy, cerebrospinal fluid leaks, therapy with alkylating agents, antimetabolites, radiation, or high-dose, long-term corticosteroids	Diabetes, heart disease, chronic pulmonary disease, chronic alcoholism	Asplenia (including elective splenectomy and terminal complement component deficiencies)	Chronic liver disease, chronic disease, recipients of clotting factor concentrates	Kidney failure, end-stage renal disease, recipients of hemodialysis	Human immunodeficiency virus (HIV) infection	Healthcare workers
Tetanus, diphtheria, pertussis (Td/Tdap)*	1-dose Td booster every 10 yrs / Substitute 1 dose of Tdap for Td							
Human papillomavirus (HPV)	3 doses for females through age 26 yrs (0, 2, 6 mos)							
Measles, mumps, rubella (MMR)*			1 or 2 doses					
Varicella*		2 doses (0, 4–8 wks)						2 doses
Influenza*	1 dose annually			1 dose annually		1 dose annually		
Pneumococcal (polysaccharide)	1–2 doses		1–2 doses					1–2 doses
Hepatitis A*	2 doses (0, 6–12 mos, or 0, 6–18 mos)		2 doses (0, 6–12 mos, or 0, 6–18 mos)		2 doses	2 doses (0, 6–12 mos, or 0, 6–18 mos)		
Hepatitis B*	3 doses (0, 1–2, 4–6 mos)		3 doses (0, 1–2, 4–6 mos)			3 doses (0, 1–2, 4–6 mos)		3 doses (0, 1–2, 4–6 mos)
Meningococcal	1 dose		1 dose		1 dose			1–2 doses

*Covered by the Vaccine Injury Compensation Program. NOTE: This schedule should be read along with the footnotes, which can be found at www.cdc-gov/nip/recs/adult-schedule.htm.

For all persons in this category who meet the age requirements and who lack evidence of immunity (e.g., lack documentation of vaccination or have no evidence of prior infection)

Recommended if some other risk factor is present (e.g., on the basis of medical, occupational, lifestyle, or other indications)

Contraindicated

NOTE: These recommendations must be read along with the footnotes, available at **http://www.cdc.gov/vaccines/recs/schedules/adult-schedule.htm.**

*Covered by the Vaccine Injury Compensation Program.

Approved by the Advisory Committee on Immunization Practices, the American College of Obstetricians and Gynecologists, the American Academy of Family Physicians, and the American College of Physicians

234

Index

Recommendations, Alphabetical by Topic

AHRQ's Electronic Preventive Services Selector (ePSS)

Bringing the prevention information clinicians need—recommendations, clinical considerations, and selected practice tools—to the point of care.

The ePSS helps you identify and select customized screening, counseling, and preventive medication services based on specific patient characteristics.

Available at
http://epss.ahrq.gov/